What people are say

A Secret History of Christianity

In this remarkable and timely book Mark Vernon helps us to recover a lost tradition in the Christian faith. At a time when the outer forms of Christianity seem to be in a state of exhaustion and confusion, he recalls us to an inner experience of Christ, a call to transformation of both vision and consciousness. In doing so he brings back into central focus neglected thinkers like Owen Barfield, poets and mystics like Blake and Traherne. He offers us a movement from the outer to the inner, from discourse about faith to a lived sense of the inner life of the Kingdom.
Malcolm Guite, Poet and author of *Mariner*, the biography of Samuel Taylor Coleridge

This is a book I wish I had written. Mark Vernon offers a forensic diagnosis of the Church's ills and invites us to recover an authentic and life-giving Christianity.
Angela Tilby, *Church Times* columnist, author, and Canon Emeritus of Christ Church, Oxford

Mark Vernon's *A Secret History of Christianity* introduces us to two individuals whom he eloquently argues embody a vital, creative response to the spiritual malaise of our time. One we have heard of and think we know, the other is practically unknown. Their names are Jesus Christ and Owen Barfield. The Jesus you'll find in this urgent, thoughtful work may surprise you, but the real surprise is Barfield. Why isn't such an insightful and necessary thinker better known? Vernon answers that question and among other things shows that by getting to know Barfield we may get to know a rather different Jesus too.
Gary Lachman, author of *Lost Knowledge of the Imagination* and *Dark Star Rising*

Running as the golden thread through Mark Vernon's remarkable panorama of Christianity are the extraordinary heterodoxies of Owen Barfield, last of the Inklings and in some ways the greatest. In this thrilling overview Vernon explores how the fulcrums in the history of human consciousness lead to radical deployments in our cosmogonies. Crucial to this is the sweep of human imagination and here Barfield joins hands with the other Inklings in their insistence that beyond our mundane sphere lie far richer worlds invisible.
Simon Conway Morris, Professor of Palaeobiology, University of Cambridge

Mark Vernon's *A Secret History of Christianity* rescues Owen Barfield from undeserved obscurity in the shadows of J.R.R. Tolkien and C.S. Lewis but in the process does so much more than that. By tracking Barfield's careful attention to how words are used and what they say about the users, he lifts our eyes, expands our horizons and reintroduces imagination into our shared religious life. We are richer for reading him – and Barfield – and listening carefully to what they have to say.
Nick Spencer, author of *The Evolution of the West*, and Research Director, Theos

In this fascinating study, Mark Vernon reminds us of the often overlooked truth of the Christian faith – that it is not there to inform us but to form us. Introducing us to the thought of Owen Barfield and the need for mystics in a flat time, this is a celebration of the "wholespeak" of poetic belief and not the "narrowspeak" of so much that peddles itself as religion in our day. The secret is, as Mother Maria Skobtsova said, "Either Christianity is fire or there is no such thing."
Mark Oakley, Dean, St John's College, Cambridge

A Secret History of Christianity

Mark Vernon has bravely stepped forward to point out what my grandfather called the taboo subject of our era; namely that people's experience of being alive evolves over time and that the pivotal moment of human evolution was two millennia ago. He invites us to step up and share the bigger view of incarnational awareness. From this new perspective, the secret history of Christianity is revealed.
Owen A. Barfield, Grandson of Owen Barfield

Mark Vernon provides fresh insights into the role of Judaism, ancient Greek philosophy, Jesus Christ, Church history, mysticism and imagination in the evolution of Western consciousness. His book gives an intriguing new perspective on where we are today. A brilliant overview.
Rupert Sheldrake, PhD, biologist and author of *The Science Delusion*

A Secret History of Christianity

Jesus, the Last Inkling, and the Evolution of Consciousness

A Secret History of Christianity

Jesus, the Last Inkling, and the Evolution of Consciousness

Mark Vernon

Winchester, UK
Washington, USA

JOHN HUNT PUBLISHING

First published by Christian Alternative Books, 2019
Christian Alternative Books is an imprint of John Hunt Publishing Ltd.,
No. 3 East St., Alresford, Hampshire SO24 9EE, UK
office@jhpbooks.com
www.johnhuntpublishing.com
www.christian-alternative.com

For distributor details and how to order please visit the 'Ordering' section on our website.

ISBN: 978 1 78904 194 1
978 1 78904 195 8 (ebook)
Library of Congress Control Number: 2018950265

A CIP catalogue record for this book is available from the British Library.

Design: Stuart Davies

UK: Printed and bound by CPI Group (UK) Ltd, Croydon, CR0 4YY
US: Printed and bound by Thomson-Shore, 7300 West Joy Road, Dexter, MI 48130

Contents

Previous books

The Idler Guide to Ancient Philosophy (Idler Books: 2015)
Carl Jung: How to Believe (Guardian Shorts: 2013)
Love: All That Matters (Hodder Education: 2013)
God: The Big Questions (Quercus: 2012)
God: All That Matters (Hodder Education: 2012)
How to Be an Agnostic (Palgrave Macmillan: 2011)
The Good Life (Hodder Education: 2010)
The Meaning of Friendship (Palgrave Macmillan: 2010)
Plato's Podcasts: The Ancients' Guide to Modern Living (Oneworld: 2009)
Dictionary of Beliefs and Religions (Editor in Chief) (Chambers Harrap: 2009)
Teach Yourself Humanism (Hodder Education: 2008)
Wellbeing (Acumen: 2008)
42: Deep Thought on Life, the Universe and Everything (Oneworld: 2008)
What Not to Say: Finding the Right Words at Difficult Moments (Weidenfeld and Nicolson: 2007)
Business: The Key Concepts (Routledge: 2002)

I will utter things which have been kept secret since the foundation of the world.

Matthew 13:35

The Christian of the future will be a mystic or he will not exist at all.

Karl Rahner

Consciousness is not a tiny bit of the world stuck onto the rest of it. It is the inside of the whole world.

Owen Barfield

Acknowledgements

I am hugely indebted to many people over many years but I would particularly like to thank those who read the manuscript in various drafts and offered often invaluable critiques, in particular Malcolm Guite, Madeleine Bunting, Rupert Sheldrake, Patrick Morrow, Brian Mountford, Jessica Kingsley, Mark Booth, Jeremy Naydler, Robert Rowland Smith, Nick George and Jules Evans. I would also like to express my sincere thanks to the Temenos Academy, which offers talks and reading groups that fully understand Barfield's notion of participation and that I have found transformative.

Introduction

Something is going wrong with Christianity. In the western world, it's not hard to make the case that something's gone terminally wrong. People are abandoning churches in their droves or, more commonly, simply steering clear of the services that nourished their forebears. In spite of sustained attempts to reverse the decline, and notable exceptions to the rule, nothing seems able to stop it.

This book is a response to the crisis, though it differs from others. It focuses on the inward aspect of Christianity's troubles. It approaches the problem at a felt or mystical level.

The root issue, I believe, lies with how Christianity has come to be presented or, to be more precise, how religious Christians have come to misunderstand the message. What was once experienced as a pathway to more life has, today, morphed into a way of life that to outsiders seems self-evidently deluded, defensive or distorted. The almost limitless capacities of the human soul, which in the past have been articulated and explored by Christianity's key exponents, as they have by the adepts of other traditions, have been largely forgotten by Christians today, and sometimes actively rejected. The upshot is that the working assumption of many western people is that Christianity will curtail your options, not expand your life, let alone affirm the truth about yourself. The people whom sociologists call "spiritual but not religious" and "nones" shrink from it.

It's tragic and, in my view, most Christian apologetics haven't really understood the nature of the problem. It's why more evangelical writers try to sell or prove, not learn and grow. It's why more liberal writers tend to cut Christianity back, feeling they must conform to, not test, contemporary secular assumptions. Both wings whittle away the secret sense of life to which the historical Jesus was clearly supremely alert.

By "secret," I don't mean a Dan Brownish reference to an occult code, let alone a conspiracy theory, but to a truth that seems obscure or hidden only because it's tricky to grasp. It's secret in the sense of being hard to see even when plainly spelt out. It's secret in the way that a buried hoard is secret though is, in truth, simply resting beneath your feet, waiting to be found. It's a perception that can be known like the quiet constancy of your breath. It's that your life springs from God's life and that this truth is yours to be discovered. It can be known directly, not on the basis of someone else's report, someone else's authority, someone else's rhetoric, but inwardly and reliably – though it's the work of a lifetime fully to align with it.

This is, in fact, standard mystical theology. It follows from the discernment that God is not another being, like you and me, but is the ground of being itself. God is known implicitly as the poetry in the poem, the fire in the equations, the life in the living, the pulse of the cosmos. And it's a truth that must be inhabited to be understood.

The situation has become critical for Christianity because over the last four or five hundred years churches have been losing touch with this inner element, which is crucial for any path that would call itself spiritual. That's happened for various reasons – the rise of science, the impact of the Reformation, the separation of psychology from spirituality. Nonetheless, it is possible to rediscover. Like the goodly pearl of great value, it's waiting to be uncovered.

* * *

I was lucky enough to find a guide in this task. He's the Oxford Inkling, Owen Barfield. He is sometimes known as the "last Inkling" because he was the last of the celebrated group to die, in 1997. A close friend of C.S. Lewis and J.R.R Tolkien, they both thought he had the most penetrating ideas. However, he wasn't as good a writer, particularly when it comes to blockbuster fiction, and so is not nearly so well known. That said, his core idea is readily understood, and radical. He has an account of our spiritual predicament that is illuminating.

It arose from a discovery. Barfield realized that the human experience of life shifts fundamentally over periods of cultural time. Our awareness of things evolves. Our consciousness changes dramatically across history.

He proposed that it happens in three phases. The first, he called "original participation" – the word "participation" referring to the felt experience of participating in life. Original participation dominates when there is little distinction between what's felt to be inside someone and what's outside because the boundaries of individual self-consciousness, which today we take for granted, are not in place. Life is therefore lived at the level of the collective. It's experienced as a continuous flow of vitality between what is "me" and "not me," between mortals and immortals, between past and present, and also between other creatures and the human creature. The inner life of the cosmos is the inner life of the people. "Early man did not observe nature in our detached way," Barfield writes. "He participated mentally and physically in her inner and outer processes."[1]

It determined life in ancient times and can sometimes be glimpsed today. It's in the waves of emotion that sweep across a crowd as, then, there's a temporary dissolution of the boundaries between the individual and others. It's an experience that's akin to stepping back in time.

A second phase away from original participation is marked by what he called a "withdrawal of participation." It happens when there's a shift from the sense of being immersed in the life of others, nature and the gods. An awareness of separation, even isolation, is felt. A person will begin to sense that they have an inner life that is, relatively speaking, their own.

Barfield argued that a momentous withdrawal of participation began to unfold in the middle of the first millennium BCE. It's the period during which quasi-scientific ideas about the cosmos began to be formed. Some humans turned away from an exclusive reliance on myths as their interests changed from sharing in life to explaining life. Questions such as the meaning of life started to appear because meaning no longer spontaneously revealed itself to such enquirers.

It was a troubling time, though, with the withdrawal of participation came an astonishing gain. The concentration of inner life that the separation from outer life brought came hand in hand with an intensification of the sense of being an individual, and with that came all manner of novel possibilities. Moral responsibility emerged, as did new relationships with deities. In the West, this moment is identified with the birth of philosophy in ancient Greece and the emergence of new religious imperatives from the Hebrew prophets. (I'm going to focus on these developments from a western perspective, though a comparable story could be told of the East.)

It's a time of awakening and rebirth and results in what Barfield called "final" or "reciprocal participation," a third phase. Now, the inner life of the individual is felt to belong to him- or herself – the gain of the withdrawal – but also to reflect the inner life of nature, the cosmos and of God. The individual has a soul that is not cut off; an interiority that can reflect and reflect on life and its meaning. People of this age have a subjectivity that can forge purposes and intentions. The awareness of participating in life still involves shared rites and ceremonies, but ideally these will be undertaken freely and consensually, not simply because a priest or a king demands it. Inwardness as we can know it is born.

* * *

Barfield's three-stage account of the evolution of consciousness is akin to what is also called the Axial Age or, as I think is more accurate, times through which "axial shifts" can be observed developing. This way of putting it was formulated by the German philosopher, Karl Jaspers. Original participation is also related to what the French ethologist, Lucien Lévy-Brühl, called *participation mystique*. Axial shifts occur when people evolve, not in the usual Darwinian sense but culturally, socio-economically, religiously and, fundamentally, existentially – in terms of their sense of themselves. It's a psychological transformation.

Where Barfield differs from axial approaches to history is that he argued these changes haven't stopped. The stages are not linear but cyclical. In fact, about five hundred years ago, western civilization embarked upon another protracted period of withdrawal. Called the Enlightenment, it has embedded the mentality of modern science and, as with previous periods of withdrawal, the developments it made possible have brought novelties. One was caught by the philosopher, Immanuel Kant, in a famous essay on the essence of this enlightenment. "Dare to know!" he declared to be the clarion call for the scientific age. However, this daring has led to many troubles taking hold of the western soul. A key one is the so-called "death of God," the widespread sense that, in truth, we may be drifting through empty, meaningless space, both literally across the cosmos, and metaphorically in our minds.

It's the predicament with which Christianity now wrestles, as do other wisdom traditions, and Barfield's analysis and its application show a way that this might be more skillfully done. The aim of my secret history is to show how, through imaginatively engaging with him, as well as testing his ideas against the findings of recent scholarship, he offers an invaluable diagnosis of the malaise of our times and, further, how the latest withdrawal may actually be part of a divine process that can still be progressed. I believe his insights can help make sense of Christianity not only to those who faithfully, if somewhat uncertainly, still go to church, but also, potentially, to the many who increasingly recoil from it.

* * *

Barfield made his discovery about the evolution of consciousness through the study of words. Philology showed him how words change meaning over time and can be treated, therefore, as fossils of consciousness. They record how minds experienced life differently in previous periods, much as the fossils of shells and bones record how bodies worked differently in previous periods.

An example is illuminating. Consider the words "wind" and "spirit." It turns out that in ancient Greek, as in many other old languages, there is a single word that means both "wind" and "spirit." It's *pneuma* in Greek and it's a relic from previous times. It's a linguistic fossil from the undifferentiated consciousness of original participation because back then, the material world mingled with the immaterial; outer with inner; mortal with immortal; wind with spirit. One word captured what we now think of as two distinct things. It's why, today, verses like John 3:8, "the *pneuma* blows where it wishes," are almost impossible to translate.

More broadly, consider the Bible as a whole. It reflects the same change from the early phase of original participation because its many words have arisen from human experiences that stretch across more than 1000 years of evolution. It is, on this reading, a fascinating assembly of consciousness fossils, and an analysis of them supports Barfield's conjecture. It shows that the New Testament is markedly more concerned with introspection than the Old Testament as would be expected, because the New Testament was written many hundreds of years after original participation and after, therefore, the emergence of a relatively autonomous inner life. Further, the words used by Augustine, three hundred years after the New Testament was written, are significantly more introspective again, because by then a phase of reciprocal participation had thoroughly bedded down.[2] In other words, the Bible and the writings of other early Christian authors carry the imprint of the shifts of consciousness that Barfield identified.

He wasn't the first to notice it. Thinkers as diverse as the British utilitarian, Jeremy Bentham, and the American transcendentalist, Ralph Waldo Emerson, had done so before. Where he differed is in arguing that Christianity played a pivotal role in the development of human awareness. It has been so central to life in the western world because the life of Jesus - and what another key interlocutor for Barfield, Rudolf Steiner, called "the Mystery of Golgotha" - captured a crucial juncture in it. Jesus can be said to have understood that the evolution of consciousness had reached a decisive moment. He embodied this moment in his life and worked it out to the full, and thereby became a forerunner that others learnt to follow. He launched the period of reciprocal participation that ran from the first millennium CE until the end of the Middle Ages. The heart of what he showed is the mystical truth, the secret: individuals are free to know in themselves that their life and God's life is one life.

It became possible to awaken to this sense of things because of what had been unfolding in the centuries prior to Jesus' time. In both the Jewish and the Greek worlds, the spiritual geniuses of the first millennium BCE had seen that the way in which people participated in life was shifting. It meant that, whereas in the periods captured by the earliest stories of the Bible and the early myths of the Greeks, people experienced themselves as members of tribes and city-states, living under the influence of the local gods and deities, by the time of the Hebrew prophets and the Greek philosophers, some were seizing hold of another experience. They awoke to an interiority that had a life of its own. They also began to develop different perceptions of the divine.

I'll track this process in the first four chapters. It has relevance not only as history but as the backdrop for our perceptions and participation.

The unfolding did not stop there. The prophets and sages began to feel that the full implications of these subtle shifts had to be incarnated. To be wholly realized, the inside of the cosmos needed to be manifested not just in the ideas of perceptive teachers but in the life of an individual. Only then, could the process of separating out the inner life of human beings from the inner life of nature turn, like a tide, and become a process of reconnecting human minds with the world and the divine. This individual would demonstrate that what comes into a person from outside cannot fundamentally affect them anymore, but instead what matters is what dwells in their hearts, and so comes out in their lives. He or she would need to project a felt sense of what it is to possess a mind that knows of a kingdom of infinite space not only above but also within. Such an individual would need not to teach others, but show them by embodying it. They would be a revelation of how someone can be fully human and fully transparent to God.

In his life, Jesus became such a central figure in the West, the individual around whom is marked nothing less than the turn of the millennia, because his life was this revelation. He crystalized such a perception of what it means to be human, the perception with the potential for a consciousness of individuality as made in the image of God.

Chapters five and six unpack this understanding of Jesus and examine his teaching, life practices, death and resurrection through this lens. It's not an exclusive account – his life will always exceed any one telling – but it is different from what is commonly heard in churches, at least in my experience. It's not about how "Jesus saves," to cite the trite formulation of our times that I believe puts so many people off, but rather is about how Jesus initiates a way that can become our own. It's about how

Jesus invited his followers to take up their cross and work out their own salvation so that they, too, might know the mystery of life in all its fullness.

The next chapter explores how this was known in the medieval period, and then finally we come to how consciousness evolved again into the modern period. It is marked by a second, major withdrawal from a felt connection with nature and the divine. It's produced the gains of science and technology, and a further valuing of the individual. But it's also led to the problems of our age. So, in the last chapter, I come to what this way of looking at things can mean for us. At heart, it is that we can develop the skills of the mystics once more and actively align to a level of life that was appealing, even obvious to our ancestors, and can become so again. We can gain a form of reciprocal participation right for our times.

New sight emerges across the course of time, Barfield argued. Our awareness of life changes. This development is painful, though the struggle often reveals gifts. It shatters limited horizons. It enables us imaginatively to perceive the vitality of divine reality afresh, and once more participate in it.

Chapter 1

The Early Israelites

The secret history of Christianity has a long prehistory. It has two ancient strands – one Hebrew, one Greek – and we'll begin with the first. Take the earliest archaeological evidence that there was a tribe called Israel. It's immediately suggestive of how different their consciousness of themselves was from ours.

The evidence is an inscription written into the Merneptah Stele, a granite slab that was found in the ruins of ancient Thebes. Dating from the reign of a thirteenth-century BCE Egyptian pharaoh, it memorializes a confrontation. The conflict was between the great civilization of the Nile, which by then was already close to two millennia old, and a younger tribe of hill people who lived in northern Palestine. "Israel is laid waste and his seed is not," it reads.

Pharaoh's army had attacked Israel, presumably because it troubled the valuable trade routes that ran between Egypt and Mesopotamia. It's known from other sources that capture and removal was deployed by the Egyptians in the late centuries of the second millennium as a way of neutralizing trouble spots. The policy may well lie behind the stories of Moses and the exodus as well as the biblical "novella" that tells of the fortunes of Joseph, who was kidnaped and taken to the land of the black soil and sun (Genesis 37–50).

The Israelite hill people were followers of Abraham, Isaac and Jacob, the fathers of an ancient clan lineage. Back then, these names would have carried immense power. As a Bronze Age community, they would have felt them not as dead patriarchs but present realities. The names conveyed a felt rootedness to the land and a spirited belonging with their god. The Bible echoes this vitality when it points out that "Abraham" carries the meanings of "exalted ancestor" and "ancestor of a multitude" (Genesis 17:5).

Pharaoh's declaration of his victory over Israel was as much a boast or a warning as a report. Israel's seed clearly wasn't terminated. And in this seeming exaggeration, Egypt was engaged in a common feature of these times. Ancient people reveled in their triumphs, and they did so in a particular way: by amplifying the bloodshed.

The first Israelites did it, too. In line with the received wisdom, they saw their conquests as an outflow of divine justice. The accounts of slaughter were experienced as restoring a right relationship between gods and peoples, and they showed little or no concern for those who were slain. Justice then meant cosmic balance not personal rights. There was no conception of the individual who might have rights. It's another example of the experiential gap between then and now, and how ancient people's perception of life was dramatically dissimilar to our own. It means that nowadays it can be profoundly uncomfortable to read some sections of the Hebrew Bible.

The perception was linked to the way in which they shared their experience of life with the life of the land and of the deities who dwelt in the land, not least on sacred mountains. The divine saga was their saga; nature's life was their life; its story was theirs.

Take Psalm 125. In modern translation, it begins: "Those who trust in the Lord are like Mount Zion, which cannot be moved, but abides forever. As the mountains surround Jerusalem, so the Lord surrounds his people, from this time on and for evermore." The psalmist turns to the mountains that encircle Jerusalem, and the holy Mount Zion in particular. In front of him, he sees the source of his strength. He is not celebrating an inner resilience, hidden within, and composing metaphors to assert it, as we might do today, but is instead straightforwardly assured by Judea's sacred geography. He doesn't have an inwardness that is separate. He identifies with his god, place and people. It is as if he sings: I am safe because I am in Judea, and in Judea is Jerusalem, and surrounding Jerusalem are the mountains where God dwells.

Alternatively, consider what may be the oldest biblical reference to Israel, found in the Song of Deborah (Judges 5). It's a victory hymn that comes from about the same time as the Merneptah Stele. It includes the memorable detail of Jael, the wife of Herber, using a mallet to drive a tent peg into the head of Sisera, an enemy commander (Judges 5:24–27). But alongside the violence comes an exuberant celebration of the god and land that the Israelites took to be on their side.

When they marched against their Canaanite foes, they felt that this god was marching with them: "Lord, when *you* went out from Seir," they sang (Judges 5:4, my italics). His presence was known to them not because they felt brave or just in their cause, as an embattled group might today, but because the earth trembled and the heavens opened, pouring forth life-giving water (Judges 5:5). The surrounding mountains, which is to say the nearby deities, fearfully acknowledged the advance, too. They "quaked before the Lord, the One of Sinai, before the Lord, the God of Israel" (Judges 5:4). And then, during the battle, the stars in heaven fought for Israel, as did the waters of the River Kishon. It disgorged a torrent that swept the enemy away (Judges 5:20–21).

Such experiences of divine entities fighting enemies in alliance with human warriors are common in stories from other ancient cultures that share this type of consciousness. In the *Iliad*, Homer describes Achilles's fight with the river-god, Scamander. The watery deity was on the side of the Trojans and repeatedly tried to kill the Greek hero from the waves. Or consider again how ancient Egypt celebrated its triumphs. Amongst the ancient inscriptions at Luxor are those that describe the famous battle of Kadesh, in which Ramesses II fought the Hittites. They, too, deploy "mythic history," as Jeremy Naydler calls it.[3] For instance, they commemorate the battle taking place at night, which in practice probably didn't happen because ancient generals preferred the daylight, though the inscriptions are not a piece of clumsy misreporting. Rather, they're an attempt to express how human affairs are reflections of timeless encounters between gods, in this case the victory of the sun god Ra over the serpent-god, Apophis. Apophis is the enemy of the divine sun. Hence, at a mythical level, the battle of Kadesh took place before a new dawn, which is to say that, by the wisdom of the times, it is more correct to report that the conflict occurred at night.

This points to a further difference between then and now. You could say that if time is a unit of measurement for us, time was a playing field of heavenly conflicts and purposes for them. Instead of working out what had happened, they worked out what things meant. That depended upon insightful mythological explanations, not good evidential support. The story that was told was shaped by the prophetic discernment of outward signs, not the weighing up of hard facts. As is sometimes noted by biblical scholars, Israel's god is presented as a "lord of history" so that "whatever happened was ultimately Yahweh's doing," as Michael Coogan explains.[4] The old tales are interpreted, therefore, as attempts to fathom what Yahweh was up to, and why. It was a natural and spontaneous way to gain understanding. Mythic history was not fanciful history but true history, as ancient peoples saw it.

* * *

What was remembered, and the way in which it was remembered, illustrates the type of awareness that people then had. If that's accepted then the concepts and judgments that shape our sense of things can be put to one side, and the ancient world can re-emerge. It becomes possible to tune into an older form of consciousness, at least to some extent. The Old Testament can take on powers akin to those of poetry, dislodging the assumptions of our age to disclose an experience of god and place that's half forgotten. The epics and narratives have an inner life and can facilitate an expansion of our awareness of the divine, insofar as we can imaginatively refocus and connect with them.

It's why biblical stories and prophecies still feel enriching to read and study, though often simultaneously disorientating and troubling. They are powerfully evocative, opening upon not only the prehistory of Christianity but the prehistory of our minds. Jews know it when they recite the tale of the exodus not in a seminar but in the context of the Seder, accompanied by ritual blessings and special food. Christians know it when they hear a recitation in a dark cathedral, before sunrise, at the dawn service of Easter. The setting helps to recapture something of original participation.

* * *

The Bible preserves myths and memories that, read aright, can reignite. Take a single verse that has been dated back to the earliest oral traditions of the prehistoric period: "A wandering Aramean was my father" (Deuteronomy 26:5). It's known to be old because the name "Aram" was found in a non-biblical text from the eighteenth century BCE, implying that what is now the biblical verse could echo back to 2000 BCE or more. The phrase, "A wandering Aramean was my father" is, therefore, another fossil in words. It transmits something of the experience of semi-nomads from the Fertile Crescent. It is intimately connected to the story of Abraham leaving the city of Ur. The phrase could have become a kind of incantation, with the power to bond the Israelite tribesmen who lived under the name. I think it would have felt as if it had been given to them. Working from the outside in, they would have absorbed this experience of belonging into themselves. It could, thereby, forge a collective sense of the people's self.

A recognition of this type of pooled identity can make sense of the early traditions surrounding Moses, too. He was another figure whose living name grew and grew as knots of meaning were continually added to it. In a world of oral memory, his story gathered together and organized perhaps several tales of Egyptian enslavement, exodus and liberation. In the mentality of the era, the name came to carry enormous theological weight. It could convey what had happened as a sign of celestial victory, as well as memorializing the terrestrial suffering and struggle.

The method is embedded in another old pericope, now recorded at Exodus 15:20, the song of Miriam: "Sing to the Lord, for he has triumphed gloriously: horse and rider he has thrown into the sea." It is one more fossil phrase, as if given out of divine time. With it, more insights into divine activity could be uncovered. It's not that the facts would become firmer, but that the implications richer. The Israelites, along with other ancient peoples, were embedded in such an experience of life. They had no perception of the this-worldly criteria that so intensely inform what we make of things now.

* * *

The early gods of Israel were also known through these multidimensional cross-currents of experience and event, which is why scholars today stress that there is not one religion or theology in the Bible, but a superposition of many. It couldn't be otherwise. The research shows that the deities who formed the lives of the first early Israelites were not singular or simply identified with Yahweh. Solomon's temple, for example, clearly contained altars to Baal, Asherah and others (2 Kings 23:4).

It was only subsequently that this became a scandal, when Yahweh was adopted as a favored protector-deity by the first kings of Israel and Judah, around 1000 BCE, and then, as ninth-century BCE prophets like Elijah and Elisha championed a "Yahweh-alone" movement. Before then, most people's experience of the divine was inherently plural and dispersed. Gods were encountered as diffuse presences associated with various mythologies, different times of the year, and assorted sacred places.

Some were felt day by day. They make an appearance in Genesis 31:19, in the form of the clan deities that Rachel steals from Laban the Aramean in a bid to gain the upper hand in a local dispute. These are the gods of the ancestors. They were attended to at the fire of the encampment, the natural focus for offerings and prayers, as is still half-caught in the intimate phrase "hearth and home."

Another set of deities were those associated with sacred locations, like Mount Zion. This category of gods known to the early Israelites included a number mentioned in the Bible, such as El, Baal, Asherah, Ishtar, and Yahweh. I think you can go so far as to say that a tribe of the time would have known they were in a different place not only by changes in the landscape and geography but by changes in the gods who manifested themselves as they traveled. It's another experience implicitly acknowledged in the Bible. "When the Most High [Elyon] apportioned the nations, when he divided humankind, he fixed the boundaries of the peoples according to the numbers of the gods" (Deut 32:8). It may explain why the Israelites developed the practice, in their periods of wandering, of carrying a tabernacle. A portable altar was an innovative way of keeping one particular divine presence with them.

A few of the old gods stood out. "El," for example, means "high god." So, when Jacob had a vision of a ladder reaching between earth and heaven, at the top of which he saw "the Lord," he assumed that he had seen El (Genesis 28:13). In time honored fashion, he raised a stone to commemorate the revelation, remarking that the Lord is in this place, and therefore naming it, "House of God," Bet-El or Bethel (Genesis 28:18–19). Similarly, Baal can mean "master" or "lord," and Yahweh "the one who is" – a meaning that was to become overwhelmingly important from the eighth century BCE onwards. But before that perception developed, the many gods reigned and they formed a pantheon. "God [Elohim] has taken his place in the divine council; in the midst of the gods he holds judgment," says Psalm 82:1.

The importance of sacred places for this mode of consciousness is reflected in another way, in the significance the Bible gives to one particular place, Mount Horeb. Also called Mount Sinai, it is the location for what appear to be at least two theophany traditions. The first is that of Moses, featuring a bush on Mount Horeb that burned without being consumed (Exodus 3:2). The second is that of Elijah and the peak of Mount Horeb. There is no burning bush, but instead an experience "of sheer silence" (1 Kings 19:12). Stephen Geller argues that Horeb-Sinai was recognized as a place where deity dwelt. "Horeb is said to have 'burned with fire to the heart of heaven,'" he notes.[5] The place spoke of God, so it was natural that Moses and Elijah were remembered as going there. At Horeb-Sinai, the people of Israel realized just how thoroughly their life was connected with this divine life.

There's a deeper insight, here, one that is crucial to the way consciousness was subsequently to evolve. Back then, there could be no monotheistic perception of God because it takes the focused mind of an individual to apprehend it and, as we've seen, people of such eras did not experience life as singular individuals. The experience of deity was inevitably scattered because that was how human beings experienced themselves. They lived in flows of divine activity that moved through them and moved them about. They were waves on a cosmic sea. I suspect this is the fundamental reason why the radical monotheism of Pharaoh Akhenaton, in the fourteenth century BCE, faded as quickly as it flared. No one knew quite what to make of the idea that there is only one God, which he called the Aten, including the visionary pharaoh himself. So, upon his death, beliefs reverted back to a nuanced form of pantheism.[6]

* * *

Things began to change a little when, at the turn of the first millennium BCE, the Israelites sought another source of collective empowerment. It was one already deployed by the great civilizations that surrounded them: divine monarchs. The evidence suggests that two regions in Canaan formed into two kingdoms, Israel and Judah, probably under the relentless pressure of having to defend themselves from circling superstates like Egypt. Kings brought the gain of strengthening the tribes. The Bible remembers these two regions being temporarily united under the leadership of David and Solomon, before splintering again and being ruled over the next few centuries by a succession of northern and southern kings.

The new monarchs modeled themselves on the pattern of a covenantal relationship between the local high god, the king and the people. It was typical of Near Eastern nations. It's why David brought the ark of God to Jerusalem. It established a royal theology as the cornerstone of his power (2 Samuel 6:17). Solomon, likewise, built a high temple that became the cultic focus for the people of Judah, a place where their god indisputably dwelt and where the glory could be experienced. The kings were knitting together deity, land, city, monarch, glory and blessing, and thereby secured the people's devotion. As Robert Bellah describes it: "God's chosen king, in the temple, on the holy mount, in the sacred city, in the land that, by extension, can as a whole be called Zion."[7] The kings of Zion promised that, as inhabitants of Zion, the people would know who they were. It's another form of collective identity, reinforced by the monarch.

God's presence could now be transmitted through them as they were divine appointees. To venerate the king was to venerate the mediator of heavenly realms. Sections of the Bible that reach back to this era go so far as to call the king "God," at least on one occasion: "Your throne, O God [addressing the king], endures for ever and ever ... Therefore God, your God, has anointed you" (Psalm 45: 6–7). They also describe kings as begotten by God, the firstborn of God, and seated at the right hand of God. That is no surprise under original participation. Much as a mountain was a place where a god dwelt, and a temple rite or idol could awaken one to the presence of a god, so a king possessed a divine aura. It's an experience still half-felt today when a monarch is crowned. The diadem that is placed upon the royal head is circular like the Sun and usually decorated with foliate elements, echoing the Sun's coronal rays. In being crowned, the monarch is being identified with the supreme icon provided by nature of the divine. The royal presence similarly radiates.

It was for this reason that the prophets of Israel, who had begun to emerge at this time, too, were nervous of kingship and, in Israel at least, kings were never unanimously accepted. A divine monarch might usurp the place of God in the people's hearts and affections and, as was also stressed at the time, what protection could a relatively minor monarch hope to afford against the mighty kings of Egypt, Assyria and, later on, Babylon? For pragmatic and for pious reasons, the first prophets argued that it is better to rely directly on the ancient deity, Yahweh, and they were wont to mock the protection offered by mere kings. The upshot was that Yahweh's centrality for Israel and Judah began to be stressed.

In conjunction with this, something else began to be felt, as well, because kingship stirred an awareness within the people. They could begin to think of themselves as subjects. It's still a collective sense of self, one that works from the outside in, though it has a different focus to a deity or mountain. Identity is now found in the form of a living person, a visible king.

It's also an unstable sense of self because monarchs, being human not mountains, are inevitably vulnerable. They die, which is why when one reign comes to an end it's crucially important quickly to establish the next and maintain the royal succession. But this mix of stability and instability, coupled to the new sense of being a subject, proved to be immensely fruitful for the evolution of monotheism. It nurtured the perception and value, first, of a divine king, and then, second, the possibility that the real king of Israel might not be the man sat upon the throne but Yahweh himself – the deity on the eternal throne of heaven that is established forever, and so not subject to the transience of human life.

This transcendent sense deepened when, about 300 years after the establishment of the monarchies, their inherent political weakness became critical. A crisis was precipitated that wasn't just civic and social but existential and theological. It led to what scholars think of as the second broad period of ancient Jewish history. It's the one in which original participation began to be left behind and a consciousness more like our own took hold. It was to become crucial for Christianity.

* * *

It was a revolution, and it began in the middle of the eighth century. Prophets like Amos and Hosea began definitively to realize that the monarchies were failing to deliver on their promise of security. They had substantial reason to do so. The neo-Assyrian empire, another of the superpowers that surrounded Israel, had recently revived in a terrifying and astonishing manner. The new king, Tiglath-Pileser III, adopted policies that reflected unprecedented military might, longer bureaucratic reach, and a freshly concentrated theocratic vision. Instead of making conquered peoples vassals, and offering protection in return for loyalty, he incorporated them directly into the state. To ensure loyalty, he deported the indigenous ruling classes and, in their place, installed his own men. In 738 BCE, he seized an opportunity when Jeroboam III of the northern kingdom of Israel died. He marched into the country and mercilessly subdued it.

The southern kingdom of Judah escaped the round of campaigning possibly because its capital, Jerusalem, was tucked away in inaccessible highlands. It was a reprieve that felt exhilarating to some, not least the prophet Isaiah who interpreted the events as divine favor. He sang of the future he felt it foretold.

> In days to come the mountain of the Lord's house shall be established as the highest of the mountains, and shall be raised above the hills; all nations shall stream to it ... For out of Zion shall go forth instruction, and the word of the Lord from Jerusalem ... The haughtiness of people shall be humbled, and the pride of everyone shall be brought low; and the Lord alone will be exalted on that day. (Isaiah 2:2,3,17)

His words were a bit of a mixed blessing. Politically, they were noble insofar as he also envisaged swords being beaten into ploughshares and spears into pruning hooks (Isaiah 2:4). But they were also high risk. By so fulsomely magnifying Yahweh, he was flirting with disaster and playing with the lives of his contemporaries. The Assyrians and the Assyrian gods were bound to be offended.

Further, alongside the declarations of Zion's height and Yahweh's triumph, his message carried a worrying undertone. At about the same time, Isaiah had a vision of Yahweh in the temple. What struck him about the revelation was the incomprehensible otherness of the deity he saw. "Holy, holy, holy!" he heard the angels cry (Isaiah 6:3), originally an expression not of awesome excellence but fearsome strangeness. The prophet naturally felt unclean before such a supernal entity, and when he emerged from the temple, he preached a message of bewilderment. He told the people to keep listening and not comprehending; to keep looking and not understanding (Isaiah 6:9). It was an early sign that the prophets were not simply reasserting the power of Israel's God against their enemies. They were agitating for a completely new perception of divine life, and of what it might be to be human, too.

About the same time, Amos preached a similarly perplexing mix. He declared that Yahweh hates burnt-offerings, assemblies and festivals, the practices that a consciousness shaped by original participation would assume secure a divinity's love (Amos 5:21–22). Did they not obey the instructions the kingly covenant and temple religion insisted Yahweh wanted? Wasn't their faithfulness the reason that Jerusalem had been spared? But like Isaiah, Amos attacked the sacred officials who practiced the rituals and imputed that the divine king was neither just nor righteous. Amos, too, was beginning to catch sight of a spiritual transformation.

Little wonder that Amaziah, the priest, told Amos to prophesy elsewhere (Amos 7:12). Having heard the holy man's message, he concluded that Amos must be in the wrong place because Amos was speaking in Bethel, precisely the spot where the heavenly hierarchy had been revealed to Jacob in the vision of the ladder. Amos's response must have been even more infuriating and baffling. "I am no prophet, nor a prophet's son, but I am a herdsman, and a dresser of sycamore trees," he said (Amos 7:14). He didn't know what he was talking about either. He just felt compelled to say it. "The lion has roared; who will not fear?" he added, presumably including himself (Amos 3:4).

Another prominent voice, that of Hosea, proclaimed the eighth-century combination of new revelation and baffling uncertainty in a different way. In his life, he enacted a parable that brought him nothing but distress. He felt that Yahweh required him to marry a woman called Gomer who was a sacred prostitute in the cult of Baal. This blasphemer bore him children, compounding his confusion because children are supposed to be a sign of Yahweh's blessing. The message seemed to be that his personal humiliation was a foretaste of the distress the people would undergo if they were loyal to Yahweh. "Come, let us return to the Lord," he said. "After two days he will revive us; on the third day he will raise us up, that we may live before him ... He will come to us like the showers, like the spring rain that waters the earth" (Hosea 6:1–3). The trouble was that before the spiritual rain, came the ordeal of misunderstanding and disgrace. His hearers must have wondered what on earth he was on about.

Looking back, we can see that the genius of the eighth-century prophets was to intuit that, amidst the anxieties of the age, a new consciousness of themselves and God was unfolding. What Amos and Hosea, in particular, were beginning to realize was that, as the monarchy failed, the nature of the covenant must change. It would no longer be held in the pooled identity of the kingly theocratic order. People would need to come to know Yahweh's presence in a different way. Only, at this stage, it was entirely unclear in what way.

* * *

King Hezekiah must have felt it was only wise to ignore their warnings. Like Amaziah, he presumably felt fully justified in assuming that the prophets were wrong. After all, he inherited a capital city, in 715, that had boomed in the decades since the northern kingdom's fall. What had been bad news for his neighbor appeared to be a godly blessing for him. Refugees had flooded to Jerusalem, leading to it quadrupling in size. Hezekiah seized the opportunity to centralize by housing and feeding them. In so doing, he transformed Judah from a rural kingdom to a city-state.

His conviction that Yahweh was sanctioning not questioning his actions was captured in his royal name. It means "Yahweh strengthens" and Hezekiah showed his strength in deeds as well as words. He abolished the clan cults of the countryside, and drew more power to the temple and himself. As other religious authorities told him, he was the one doing what was right in the eyes of the Lord. "He removed the high places, broke down the pillars, and cut down the Asherah. He broke in pieces the bronze serpent that Moses had made, for until those days the people of Israel had made offerings to it," the Bible reports (2 Kings 18:4).

We can imagine the battle between the conservative king and the revolutionary prophets intensifying when another tense moment arrived to test the rival pieties. A new Assyrian king, Sennacherib, ascended the throne and, in 705, he pivoted his royal eye back towards Jerusalem. Hezekiah launched a dramatic program of fortifications to withstand the expected siege and attack, the most arresting remnant of which is the half-kilometer long Siloam Tunnel, hand-cut through solid rock. It would provide the newly dependent population with water from a spring located outside of the city walls.

Then, in 701, Sennacherib marched the Assyrian war machine back into Judah. He first besieged the hill town of Lachish, constructing a ramp that survives. The town fell, was razed and, as relief carvings now in the British Museum show, the defeated were treated without mercy. They were pulled from the ramparts and impaled. A mass grave of 1500 men, women and children has been found. Those with any status who survived the pillage were loaded onto carts and deported.

Jerusalem seemed sure to fall next except that for reasons which have eluded historical explanation, Sennacherib suddenly withdrew. The city-state was spared a second time. The pro-Hezekiah interpolation was that a bloodthirsty angel of Yahweh appeared and slew 185,000 Assyrians in a single night (2 Kings 19:35). Perhaps the army was struck by a plague. Whatever the cause, Jerusalem had another escape that was again experienced as a glorious divine deliverance, further boosting Hezekiah's confidence. It seemed that the royal covenant was firmly intact. The irritating prophets had clearly been mistaken, proof of which was that Hezekiah reigned for another fifteen years and died peacefully in his bed.

But, in fact, the effects of Hezekiah's triumphant policies had unexpected side effects. Over the next few years, they were to vindicate the intuitions of Isaiah, Amos and Hosea.

* * *

Consider the impact of Hezekiah's abolition of the rural clan cults. He had launched the purge to empower the temple, but cutting the people off from their ancestors who were buried and venerated in the old sacred places had powerful implications. It severed a link between the living and the dead with the result that, as archaeological investigations show, a new practice began during Hezekiah's reign. Clan tombs were replaced by sepulchers for single burials and crypts that held just one or two generations of a family.[8]

It was a dramatic departure from the ancient burial customs that, under original participation, were as timeless as the household gods. Abraham himself was assumed to have received an old style burial when he died and was "gathered to his people," that is, was interred in ancestral ground (Genesis 25:8). But from now on, the dead of Jerusalem began to be buried in urban necropolises. "[T]he ancestral community, the kin corporation, had moved decidedly in the direction of smaller units, probably centered on the nuclear family," writes Baruch Halpern.[9] "The individual had been divorced from the clan sector."

Or perhaps it's more accurate to say that this action began to forge people into individuals, period, because when you alter burial practices, you alter basic existential perceptions. Single burials imply that a person must set out on the afterlife alone, not in the company of his or her clan. A solitary grave implies a solitary departure. The burden of responsibility for what happens in death, and therefore in life too, shifts. It no longer rests with the tribe but with a new entity: the individual. That's a fearsome prospect and a spiritual challenge. It might also lead to a transformation of awareness.

In other words, the change in burial practices exposes the heart of what it is to be a people whose perception of life is closely tied to the landscape. They had been indigenous; of particular places. Now, they were uprooted. It must have doubled the mood of sacred uncertainty projected by the prophets. And did Hezekiah himself have a moment of doubt when he decided to be buried in the traditional way (2 Kings 20:21)? Whatever the truth of that, his burial policy, by introducing a rupture with what is natural to original participation, seems to have prompted an inkling that a different kind of self-consciousness is possible, one with a markedly different, personal consciousness of self.

It became stronger with a second policy that enforced, again probably inadvertently, the dynamic of interior growth. Hezekiah encouraged literacy.[10] A surge of Hebrew texts appear in the archaeological record from this time, and stylistic changes to the Hebrew language were also introduced. They can be interpreted as evidence that the ability to read grew dramatically. It reached levels of perhaps 20 percent of the population, a remarkable fraction when compared with less than one percent that was the average across, say, ancient Egypt. Literacy was no longer confined to a tiny scribal class.

It seems that Hezekiah encouraged reading for the same reason he banned the clan cults, to secure order. Centralization and the growth of Jerusalem required new ways of maintaining social cohesion, and this was found via the creation of written narratives. The city-state might find a shared identity in these circulating sacred texts. They could bolster the older oral traditions that would have been weakened by the purge of sacred sites and traditional holy places. Only, the literacy precipitated a side effect. It, too, put a stress on the importance of the individual.

These early versions of what was to become the Bible prompted the idea of private, devotional reading. Before the reign of Hezekiah and the spread of literacy, the evidence suggests that most people would have recognized only a few isolated words when they saw them written down. These words would have been charmed names or single-line blessings, and they were treated as memorials or talismans. They have been found chiseled onto walls or inscribed on rolled-up bits of parchment, which suggests that they were worn as pendants around the neck. But with literacy emerges a different relationship to words. Literate individuals can read whole prophecies and lengthy stories, offering them the possibility of a sustained personal encounter. Though the written texts were probably designed to secure dependence upon the cult, the king and the temple, they could also be contemplated alone. A talismanic word could invoke an ancestor or god, but a lengthy bit of scripture could nurture a sense of divine presence that dwelt internally, in the heart and mind. To read, therefore, is to forge an inner life; it's to make an individual.

This was key to the psychological revolution that began to unfold. If the analysis of the evidence is right, the people of Hezekiah's reign were the generation that definitively embarked on the journey which would eventually make the people of Israel some of the greatest spiritual innovators of all time. They would stop being the people of a particular god, monarchy and place. They would, instead, become the people of a book.

Chapter 2

The Birth of the Bible

In terms of the evolution of consciousness, the emergence of written texts that are read privately is seismic. The appearance of a sacred book initiates a new religious movement. That it took several centuries to establish, bed down in people's lives and, thereby, spiritually flourish is symptomatic of the revolution. But something was unleashed in the time of Hezekiah that, ultimately, changed everything.

With increased literacy, the religious authority that had been held in the scribal class who were tied to the state grew fuzzy at the edges. Priests, who had been using writing for many centuries already, found their religious monopoly challenged. The reading of scriptures continued to be patrolled by various hierarchies, but they could not stop it spreading into the secluded space that forms between the page and the studious reader. Little wonder that individual reading, as opposed to public recitation, was long regarded with wary suspicion. It wasn't just a different way of doing things; it was a different way of being human and knowing God.

There are intimations of misgivings woven into the writings of the Bible itself. The prophet Jeremiah, who was active towards the end of the seventh century, about a century after Hezekiah's reign, makes one skeptical remark: "How can you say, 'We are wise, and the law of the Lord is with us', when, in fact, the false pen of the scribes has made it into a lie?" (Jer 8:8). The prophet goes on to imply that those who love scriptures may be unwittingly rejecting Yahweh. That's the danger of private piety.

Alternatively, there's the wry observation of the later scribal author of Ecclesiastes: "Of making many books there is no end, and much study is a weariness of the flesh" (Ecc 12:12). He was presumably warning those who were attempting religiously to go it alone. It might make you but it might equally break you.

A touching story, which was probably written down as the implications of such shifts became clearer, majors on the experience of a woman, Hannah. One day, she went to the temple and prayed silently (1 Sam 1:12). Eli the priest, a man dedicated to the old ways, saw that her lips didn't move. He was disturbed and accused her of drunkenness, until she explained what it meant. She said that she was pouring out her soul to God. She hadn't been reading, but she had been engaged in a parallel activity: communicating with God inwardly. Her interiority could somehow mysteriously connect with the interiority of God.

Plato articulated comparable concerns in the context of fourth-century BCE Athens, as his culture went through a similar transition. He voiced the fear that writing had become a tool that facilitated the forgetting of wisdom, even as it appeared to record it, because the truth of written words cannot, in fact, live on the page. Literature needs wise readers, individuals with educated hearts, and they are hard to find.

It means that scriptures create new forms of religious anxiety. How might I understand a text without an authority to guide me? And even with such an authority, how can the meaning of texts be settled? Sacred writing generates personal disquiet alongside private devotion, religious squabbles and in times to come, wars, even as it heightens truth's aura. The meaning is not quite on the page. It's not quite in the mind. So where is it? Literate people have to learn to focus and tolerate the slow disclosure of meaning. They have to develop a binocular vision that can read words and remain open for what comes through words. They have to learn to live on a virtual threshold, a dematerialized doorway to the holy of holies. It's all very different from performing the required rituals or venerating the anointed king.

Then, as now, I imagine there was a huge temptation to grasp at the literal meaning of a text and insist that it was the whole truth. A more nuanced way to read scriptures was, therefore, institutionalized from about the fifth century BCE. It drew on a distinction between written texts that can't be changed and oral commentaries on those texts, the very spirit of which is dynamic. It's enacted in the events carefully described in the book of Nehemiah, which was written at this time. The priest, Ezra, is said to have read from the sacred book of the written law, opening it in the sight of all the people, after which the Levites interpreted the text, "so that the people understood the reading" (Nehemiah 8:5–8). Reading is one thing. Understanding is its necessary complement. The purpose of the Ezra story may have been to communicate that the devout Jew must, henceforth, be both priest and Levite, reader and interpreter.

This explains the emergence of a further development: the fixing of a canon of authorized scriptures, which occurred from the fifth century onwards. It may have happened to solve another problem that arises with sacred textuality. Myths and stories in oral traditions live in the telling and retelling, as they are elaborated across various versions. Such layers of remembrance would have charged the venerable names, Abraham and Moses, with their active reality. But with writing this process becomes troublesome. The earlier versions of a written text might continue to exist alongside newer ones, and be felt to conflict with them – as indeed appears to have happened because, at first, the scribes treated written documents like oral memories. They continued extensively to edit and amend them. It's one reason for the confusing, palimpsest-nature of the Bible as we have it.

What is now called the book of the prophet Isaiah, for example, is agreed by scholars today to be the work of at least three different authors and periods. First-Isaiah (chapters 1–39) is the prophet who had the vision in the temple. But the authors of Deutero-Isaiah (chapters 40–54), and Trito-Isaiah (chapters

55–66) lived a century or more later. That causes confusion, and can undermine the impact of a text rather than develop it, which is where a canon comes in. It tries to address the problem by authorizing one version. It stops the glossing and redacting, with the added twist that it reverses the way texts work compared with oral modes of transmission. When a canon is fixed, not a jot or tittle must be altered for fear of losing the revelation the written words preserve.

The Egyptologist, Jan Assmann, has observed a further intriguing impact of a canon. When canonical literature takes hold of a culture or civilization, the religious interest in transcendent reality not located in any particular place noticeably deepens. This is always limited in the experience of gods under original participation because such deities are bound, as it were, to their sacred place or celestial body. But now, it's as if the individual, reaching for a papyrus or scroll, simultaneously reaches for a presence who exceeds location. The words invite the reader to share in the life of this placeless divinity. We, who are so used to books, easily forget that each volume on the shelf is like an infinitely patient portal that opens as words leap from the page to the eye. The process is dramatically expansive of the psyche, as well as the deity, which is why reading today is routinely celebrated as a very good thing. There's a moment of alchemy as the text comes back to life, a restoration that occurs even if the poem or prophecy or myth has lain unread for decades or years. Reading puts people in touch with the timeless. "This idea of literary or artistic immortality may be considered as a first step in the direction of transcendence or transcendental visions," Assmann writes.[11]

* * *

The years up to the 620s BCE, after the death of Hezekiah, were relatively peaceful for Judah. The Assyrian empire embarked on a spate of civil wars that destabilized it, and eventually destroyed it. It withdrew from the northern regions of Israel and, in the south, Judah became a vassal of Egypt and was mostly left to itself. No new major prophets appeared and scholars have speculated that's partly because the monarchy seemed, temporarily, to have won the argument.

But what had been quietly unfolding in the inner lives of at least some people became visible when a young, idealistic king came to the throne. He was named Josiah. A keen devotee of Yahweh, he gave fresh impetus to the work of the scribes and the culture of literacy although, as with Hezekiah, his reasons were largely conservative: to secure his kingly cult and power.

His efforts are now known as the Josian or Deuteronomic Reform. The story, as it's told in the Bible (2 Kings 22–23), is that the pious monarch sponsored a restoration of temple practices and, during some building work, a momentous discovery was made. The high priest, Hilkiah, was said to have found "the book of the law in the house of the Lord" (2 Kings 22:8). In 621, the account continues, this scripture was solemnly read out to the priests, prophets and people who had assembled to listen. Another round of religious purification was launched, leading to the destruction of more clan altars and objects dedicated to gods other than Yahweh (2 Kings 23). That's what kings do. Only this time, it wasn't just that the policies of the king inadvertently continued loosening the grip of original participation.

The Josian scribes seemed to have consciously realized that a new way of relating to God was required. During the peaceful decades that followed Hezekiah's death, the inference is that they had been working on a more developed form of sacred scripture. What they announced in 621, and wisely claimed had been discovered, was actually an inspired literary creation. Scholars today believe the text that was read before the assembled people was an early version of the book of Deuteronomy, and it resolutely looked forward, not back.

The Deuteronomists, as they are now called, had grasped what was going on. Discovering and discerning the meaning of the times, they composed a text that could take the emerging consciousness of interiority to its next step. In particular, what they wrote doubled the stress on worshipping Yahweh alone by insisting that Yahweh controlled not only what happened around Mount Zion, but that Yahweh controlled everything. Henotheism, meaning the worship of one god whilst not denying the existence of others, was on the way to becoming monotheism. The Deuteronomists contemplated a possibility that even the eighth-century prophets had not imagined. Could Yahweh be God alone?

To answer yes would be a complicated affirmation. Under original participation, it is natural to assume that nations such as Assyria are favored by their god, much as Israel is by its. When the nations fought, that was but a reflection of the primary combat in heavenly realms. But if that were not so, and Yahweh was alone in heaven, or at least celestially supreme, then what was the meaning of terrestrial war and, even more pointedly, why had the Assyrians defeated the northern kingdom? The implication would be that Yahweh had taken up arms against himself, unless another possibility could be countenanced. Maybe the northern kingdom had unwittingly betrayed its covenant with Yahweh and, as punishment, Yahweh had willed for the nation to be subdued by Tiglath-Pileser. It's an almost unbearable thought, given the violence that was unleashed when an ancient superpower marched forth.

The troubling implications of a departure from henotheism do not stop there. If the northern kingdom were to be blamed for the calamity, then how exactly had it betrayed Yahweh? What might Yahweh now require from a temple and king? Did he require a temple and king at all? And if not, then maybe, the people could be held responsible. Had even individuals been at fault? With this kind of logic, the nascent monotheism of the

Deuteronomists deepened the individualizing turn. Initiated, as if by accident a few decades previously, it now became an explicit theological agenda.

To underscore the move, the Deuteronomists returned to the tradition of Moses. He became central to the reforming narrative. It's for this reason that, in the book of Deuteronomy, Moses eclipses Abraham, Isaac and Jacob. His story sidelines the story of the hill people coming from the land of Ur, by focusing instead on the Mosaic escape from Egypt and the exodus story. That now had much more resonance.

This is not just religiously revolutionary but politically so too because, unlike David and Solomon, Moses is explicitly portrayed not as a king but as a teacher and a prophet. His authority, which became colossal, did not rest on being attached to a sacred place, building a temple, or preserving a royal cult. The Deuteronomists underlined it, first, by insisting that "no one knows his burial place to this day" (Deut 34:6) and then, secondly, by adding a stirring detail. They said that he didn't make it from Egypt to Judah, but died looking out across the Promised Land (Deut 34:5).

He was eternally separated from the sacred place, implying that he leads people out of a bondage that is as much spiritual as social, and through times of struggle in an inner wilderness as much as an actual desert. As a recognizably human actor, coping with all sorts of doubts and squabbles, his story shifts from being written in the register of mythic history to a kind of devotional or contemplative history. Bellah argues that Moses became the figurehead in "a charter for a new kind of people, a people under God, not under a king." He continues: "[W]e might see Moses as a kind of 'transitional object', as a way for people who knew only monarchical regimes to give up the king and begin to understand what an alternative regime might be like."[12]

It's a radical transition because it requires, at heart, an inner, perceptual transformation or awakening. It can only become established insofar as a change of consciousness occurs. This explains arguably the most sweeping of the interventions of the Deuteronomists. It concerns how they sought to settle, once and for all, the question of the veneration of ancestors and the worship of other gods.

There had long been a wariness of idols, observed as much in the breach as observance, as the various altars in Solomon's temple suggest. But to secure monotheism required that this rich seam of religiosity be not just controlled but fundamentally stripped out. The Deuteronomists affirmed the old concern and took things a stage further by issuing an uncompromising commandment. Henceforth, iconoclasm was to be the definitive mark of devotion to Yahweh, not rituals, not holy places. Smash the altars. Break down the pillars. "Do not bring an abhorrent thing into your house, or you will be set apart for destruction like it. You must utterly detest and abhor it, for it is set apart for destruction" (Deut 7:26). From now on, God requires not only that no images are made but that everything in the form of anything in heaven, on earth, or in the water be wrecked: "For the Lord your God is a devouring fire, a jealous God" (Deut 4:24). The command is to be free of the experience of life found in original participation and step into an entirely different mode of being.

Barfield calls it the "unlikeliest" religious injunction ever to have been received. Its absoluteness must have utterly shocked. In the enchanted cosmos of original participation, a basic experience of life is that nature reflects the divine, and the gods nature. This is pantheism. To worship representations of these gods is, therefore, an expression of faithfulness, not faithlessness. A phallic figure or erect stone, like Jacob's pillar, symbolized the divine energy that flowed during ecstatic visions. The numinosity of a sacred grove or holy mountain was obvious, highlighted by the placement of an idol. A sacred cow reminded ancient Mediterraneans of motherhood and fertility and joy.

Why wouldn't you want to make one of gold to celebrate your liberation? To venerate the image of a king was to venerate the mediator between heaven and earth.

But iconoclasm is a withdrawal of this mode of participation and it unleashes a revolutionary spiritual dynamic. God is no longer to be found on holy hills, it says. By eliminating the possibility of sharing in God's life in these domains, God must be found afresh: not in the inner life of the cosmos, but in the inner life of the devotee. God must be sought in the human heart. It's what people had begun to feel with the changed burial practices and the effect of written scriptures and it now became urgent.

The Deuteronomists were making sense of the confusion of Isaiah, Amos and Hosea. Isaiah had seen God in the temple and emerged saying that God would dull the minds of his people, would stop their ears and shut their eyes, "so that they may not look with their eyes, and listen with their ears, and comprehend with their minds, and turn and be healed" (Isaiah 6:9–10). The Deuteronomists finally understood why. They comprehended that this strange, apparently perverse, divine concealment was part of God's plan.

What the worshipper of idols misses is that the supreme deity cannot be found externally, but only internally. Idols are torn down because they draw the focus outwards, towards the many gods of nature and places. Those who make them are like them because their experience of life is, correspondingly, scattered across the holy mountains and sacred groves. Unless they withdraw from their fix on that vitality, they will not find the experience of radical transcendence that can be detected within. To echo Augustine, they had to learn to "marvel at themselves,"[13] the place that God dwells. It is in the heart and soul that a spiritual self can learn to speak, see, hear and feel the divine. As a commandment, it's unforgiving. As spiritual wisdom, it reaches for the infinite.

The imperative is captured in the most crucial passage of

the book of Deuteronomy. "Now this is the commandment," the scribes declared (Deut 6:1). "Hear, O Israel: The Lord is our God, the Lord alone. You shall love the Lord your God with all your heart, and with all your soul, and with all your might. Keep these words that I am commanding you today in your heart" (Deut 6:4–5). The personal pronoun in the text, "you," is singular in the Hebrew. The verses are addressed to the individual and can be glossed in this way: "Because Yahweh must be your one and only, you [as an individual] must correspondingly love him as one does one's beloved, with all one's heart, with all one's soul, and with all one's might."

Stephen Geller has unpacked the profundity of this Deuteronomic transformation.[14] He stresses that the passage is not actually a statement of monotheism. This didn't come quite yet, not until a couple of generations later, with Deutero-Isaiah's declaration, "beside me there is no god" (44:6). It is instead an invitation to discover monotheistic knowledge of God by forming a particular kind of relationship with the divine.

People were to focus their emergent interiority onto the one God. "The one self needed a single God to comprehend itself by projecting itself onto the new concept of divinity," Geller continues. Or to put it another way, the shift towards monotheism was not primarily about novel assertions of the divine nature, which of course doesn't in fact change, but was about the cultivation of the personality of an individual who might then perceive the singularity of the divine nature. God's oneness can only be understood via a psychic bond that forms with an individual soul, one on one.

The Deuteronomists formulated what amounts to a program that could fashion personhood. By totally attaching to the one God, someone might move beyond the confusions of the era and achieve a relationship with God that exceeded what was possible under the old rites and traditions because it must rest in a unity of self. "Even heaven and the highest heaven cannot contain you, much less this house that I have built!" Solomon, the divine king, surely never uttered, but is retrospectively said to have admitted (1 Kings 8: 27). Neither could a mountain or bronze serpent. The individual person, though, just might because God's transcendence might be felt in the depths of the fathomless soul.

The program worked because in the effort to follow it and, perhaps even more importantly, in the effort to understand it, the adherent might discover a sense of self that sees and hears.

Indicative of this aim, Deuteronomy reforms much of the ancient worldview. For example, it does away with the collective responsibility for sin, which previously had been passed onto the third and fourth generations, and requires that "children shall not be put to death for their parents; only for their own crimes may persons be put to death" (Deut 24:16). Jeremiah similarly says as much too: "In those days they shall no longer say: 'The parents have eaten sour grapes, and the children's teeth are set on edge'" (Jer 31:29). If that seems like self-evident progress to us, that's only because we have internalized a sense of individual rights which begin to become comprehendible at this time.

In a similar vein, Deuteronomy vehemently challenges the bonds of clan by insisting that the individual is under no obligation to follow the gods of his or her ancestors, or the recommendations of his or her kin. In fact, they should positively not heed such advice and instead stone brothers, children and wives who offer it (Deut 13:6–10). Jesus was to say something similar. "Let the dead bury their dead" (Luke 9:60). "Whoever comes to me and does not hate father and mother, wife and children, brothers and sisters, yes, even life itself, cannot be my disciple" (Luke 14:26). "Whoever does the will of God is my brother and sister and mother" (Mark 3:35). He was following the Deuteronomic imperative with a similarly hyperbolic style that forces a struggle to understand and nurtures the inner change that comes with the effort.

Less ferociously, but no less radically, Deuteronomy suggests the possibility that women might be regarded as individuals as well as men. They are no longer treated as parts of the family, owned and ruled by the male paterfamilias. For example, in the last of the Ten Commandments, the one about not coveting your neighbor's possessions, the wife is separated out in the Deuteronomic version. She is not on the list of possessions. She is not to be regarded as belonging to the man but belonging to herself (compare Deut 5:21 with Exodus 20:17). Female slaves are given the right of manumission too, and slaves in general are treated as individuals facing unfortunate circumstances, rather than as class of people who are slavish by nature.

The changes go on. Deuteronomy insists that each person must be educated so that they might become personally persuaded of the truth of God's law. It is no longer good enough to follow traditions. "But take care and watch yourselves closely, so as neither to forget the things that your eyes have seen nor to let them slip from your mind" (Deut 4:9). Similarly, each individual must repent of their wrongs, from the heart, not just perform the prescribed ritual actions.

If the program worked, then the most important theophany of God might finally be grasped. The Deuteronomists gave that peak experience to Moses, of course, recalling the ancient story of the angel of the Lord appearing to him in the burning bush that blazed and yet was not consumed. Moses is bamboozled by the vision, asking what it means, as Jacob had struggled, literally, when the angel of the Lord appeared to him by the Jabbok ford. Only this time, God's name is not withheld, as it had been in the older traditions. Neither is Moses's name changed, as Jacob's had been, to Israel: "For you have striven with God and with humans, and have prevailed" (Genesis 32:28).

Instead, God reveals his name to Moses. "I AM WHO I AM," God says to him (Exodus 3:14). It's the "name apart," as the medieval Jewish philosopher, Maimonides, described it, the

Tetragrammaton or secret divine designation: YHWH, Yahweh.[15]

The old revelation is entirely reimagined. It no longer refers to a warrior god who fights for his loyal followers. To the Deuteronomists, it implies a deity who transcends all factions. It doesn't refer to a god of a particular place, like El or Baal, because "I AM" is not a proper name and so can't designate a region or mountain. It can't point to a particular divine being either. Instead, it opens onto being itself. It points to the internal life of God, not to a god who is here or there, doing this or that. And this name can be participated in by every human being who has an internal life too, with eyes that see, ears that hear, throats that speak.[16]

A person who can say "I am" might share in the reality of God who is I AM. That's the new basis of human-divine connection. A deity who isn't in the fire asks that devotees kindle the light of God's presence within themselves. There, they might see God's flickerings. A deity who no longer inhabits the natural world, as a spirit-wind wafting through the garden (Genesis 3:8), must be felt within in order to be known without. The Deuteronomists were inviting the people to consider themselves as a reflection in time of the eternal I AM. A felt sense of "I am," even if transient, is a prerequisite for feeling the inner power of the divine I AM.

Barfield calls it the beginning of "spiritual selfhood," of possessing an interior cosmos. That can, in turn, become a gateway through which to return to the inner life of the external cosmos, and experience it in a very different way from its torrenting in, as had been the experience before. The awakened individual can recognize the wonder of the heavens, the earth and the waters once again. The living world can be felt to resonate with the one God in a way that parallels how the living individual knows of God's implicit presence. Nature can be experienced as speaking of God rather than itself being divine, enchanted and haunted, and God can speak through creation but not be held within creation. As the Psalmists were to celebrate, skies and seas can be regarded as God's clothing and apparel, not God's pantheistic prison. "You stretch out the heavens like a tent, you set the beams of your chambers on the waters, you make the clouds your chariot, you ride on the wings of the wind, you make the winds your messenger, fire and flame your ministers" (Psalm 104: 2–4).

Henceforth, monotheistic knowledge of God would be inextricably tied up with self-knowledge, and introspection would become a key spiritual task. We can assume that it was a move that was often not welcomed. It could be just too demanding. As Jeremiah sighed: "If I say, 'I will not mention him, or speak any more in his name', then within me there is something like a burning fire shut up in my bones; I am weary with holding it in, and I cannot" (Jer 20:9).

The highly anthropomorphic biblical image of Yahweh is caught up in this effort, too. I suspect it can be regarded as a product of the early exploration of spiritual selfhood, with its implication that something within human beings is identified with the center of the cosmos. It makes the soul the holy of holies, the sanctuary where divinity intersects with nature. If human interiority is such a spectacular mirror of God's life, then it's not surprising that God was often imagined to be as impetuous and vacillating as people can be.

But knowing God within could also ease anxieties and sustain a sense of presence that is, potentially, indestructible. "O Lord, you have searched me and known me. You know when I sit down and when I rise up; you discern my thoughts from far away ... Even before a word is on my tongue, O Lord, you know it completely" (Psalm 139:1–2, 4). And the portability of the divine presence became invaluable when the vulnerability of Judah to invasion was finally realized.

* * *

In 587 BCE, the Babylonians invaded, having taken over the Assyrian empire in 609 BCE. The kings of Jerusalem had embarked on a series of policies that thoroughly irritated King Nebuchadnezzar. So, in 587, he decided he wouldn't tolerate any further disobedience. He invaded Jerusalem and destroyed Solomon's temple. He added another five thousand of the aristocracy, military and artisans to those he had previously deported, leaving the poor and the land devastated. It's the beginning of the period of exile, when the humiliated Israelites sat down by Babylon's rivers and wept.

The heart had been ripped out of the land. With the temple gone, it seemed that there was no way of getting back to the old ways with God's chosen king, in the temple, on the holy mount, in the sacred city, in the land called Zion. However, the people were equipped to survive the trauma, spiritually speaking. This was the Deuteronomists's invaluable gift. I believe it's the reason that Judaism lives today. The people's devotion could go with them because it was held within them. And, in fact, when the Babylonians were themselves conquered by the Persians, 80 years later, and Cyrus invited the Israelites to return and rebuild the temple, it seems that most of the people did not want to make the journey back. The historical record shows that Israelites returned only in dribs and drabs over the subsequent couple of centuries.

The notion of the diaspora was born. It raised a further set of issues, not least those to do with assimilation and intermarriage, the latter practice profoundly upsetting the relatively few Israelites who wanted to return to the earlier religiosity marked by ritual and place. According to the book of Ezra, named after the eponymous pious priest, the scriptures condemned those who had not remained segregated during the exile. Ezra shamed and expelled those who had entered into mixed marriages, deeming their love as an intolerable corruption of Yahweh's will (Ezra 9:1ff).

But there were other voices. "In fact, between the fifth and the third centuries BCE, a series of literary works expressed views on segregation and intermarriage quite antithetical to those of the priestly rigorists," explains Philip Jenkins. "This includes such biblical works as Jonah, Ruth, Tobit, and Esther, all of which offer favorable accounts of neighboring peoples, while Ruth and Esther both praise mixed marriages. The Song of Solomon idealizes sexual love between an Israelite and a foreign woman. Each text, in its way, was guaranteed to offend."[16] But the aim was noble: to secure the sense of God greater than could be contained by the cult because God was contained in the heart.

* * *

Monotheism and individuality continued to develop, hand in hand. From about the fifth century onwards, some Jews began to think that there could be humans who were so translucent to the divine that they shone with God. Jews were already familiar with heavenly non-human entities who, when visiting the Earth, become godlike. Jacob's wrestling angel was one, an angel of the Lord who could also be the Lord. The old story of Abraham by the oaks of Mamre offered another incident when God might have assumed angelic form, manifest as a man. "Three men" came to Abraham and he offered them hospitality (Genesis 18:1ff). Then, when they prophesied that Abraham's wife Sarah would have a son, famously provoking Sarah to laugh, one of the strangers is renamed, "the Lord." He is distinguished from the other two, who are later confirmed as having been not the Lord, but angels.

The way in which these stories have come down to us, with their layers and shifts, suggests that the post-exilic editors were learning to discern more deeply how God's presence could show up within creation and within themselves. They were formulating a reciprocal sense of participation, the inner life of God increasingly detected in the inner life of human beings, and this is explored most radically in relation to the story of Moses, once more. It came to be thought that not only heavenly creatures might be godlike. Humans like Moses might be, too. For example, we nowadays read that, after his calling, Moses's face began to shine with God's presence (Exodus 34:29). The people saw it and were terrified. They were afraid to come near because they began to see that to come into the presence of Moses was to come into the presence of God. Moses had been addressed one to one. He now radiated I AM from within himself. He was even said to have become God to Aaron (Exodus 4:16). This must be a post-exilic addition.

Subsequent texts continue in this direction of travel. The apocryphal book of Sirach describes Moses as "equal in glory to the holy ones." A book attributed to a visionary called Ezekiel the Tragedian carries on. It places Moses on a divine throne and envisages the highest of the high angels bowing down to him. He is like God.

It's a subtle business, and it is also easy to commit the worst idolatry of all: mistaking oneself for God. Hence, alongside these monotheistic explorations, a practice began of writing God's name, YHWH, but refraining from reading it out. Instead, a lesser name was substituted, like "Lord." Reading but not uttering the name apart is a way of remembering that whilst God can be found in the human heart, God remains transcendent, beyond human grasp. It's another part of the inner consciousness that the post-exilic Israelites had to learn to tune aright.

There's perhaps an echo of this caution in the fact that the statement that individuals are made in the image of God explicitly occurs in only one place in the Hebrew scriptures: in the first chapter of Genesis, one of the youngest sections of the Bible. Most of the Jewish scriptures, probably wisely, focus on the work to understand the revelation. That is the key element in developing divine receptivity. To assert doctrine, with no knowledge of its meaning, precipitates all sorts of distortions and inflations.

The notion of being made in the image of God becomes sustained and explicit only in the intertestamental period, which is to say in the Hellenistic age, after Alexander the Great walked into Jerusalem in 331 BCE. For the rampaging Macedonian, it was a minor episode, particularly as it came just a few months after the bloody siege of Tyre, in modern-day Lebanon. That subjugation had signaled Alexander as not only a good general but a great one.

But at another level, the secret history of Christianity, 331 BCE is a seismic date. It's as important as the eighth century BCE, the Deuteronomists, and all that followed. In that year, Jerusalem passed into the orbit of Greek culture. It's a change that has led some to suggest that no non-Jew has influenced the shape of Judaism as profoundly as Alexander, which is to say that no non-Jew has so influenced the shape of the Christianity that was to come, as well. In what ways did he do so? What perceptions of life and the gods did his Greek ways bring? This takes us to the second strand of Christianity's prehistory. To these questions we now turn.

Chapter 3

The Ancient Greeks

The Greek wellspring upon which Christianity draws is as ancient as the Hebrew source. It reaches back to a period close to the time of Abraham, in the second millennium BCE. Homer wrote about the stories via which the Greeks came to celebrate these distant origins, collected together in the oral traditions now known as the *Iliad* and *Odyssey*. They looked back to the civilization of Mycenae, which had flourished before 1400 BCE. It fell for reasons unknown, and the Greeks, not unlike the early tribes of Israel, began to be known as minor players in the Mediterranean world as the first millennium BCE unfolded.

They were like the Israelites in other ways. They never achieved a great or lasting empire, as the kings of Egypt and Persia did, but instead adopted a diaspora-like approach to spreading their culture. When Greek cities sprang up around the Mediterranean, like frogs on the edge of a pond, as Plato put it, they were held together by language and ritual. They focused on developing their influence in the realm of ideas about the divine world. One of their great insights was the notion of the Word or *Logos*. It became a central plank in the understanding that Christians sensed following the life of Jesus of Nazareth. They also laid down important precursors to monotheism as philosophers made the case that godliness is akin to goodness and oneness.

Further similarities stand out. As the Greeks related stories of heroic ancestors and mythic history, and then adopted sacred writing, so they became a people of books, those of Homer and Hesiod, in particular. The significance of writing is remembered in another way. They had an alphabet comprised of 22 non-pictographic, which is to say iconoclastic, letters: *alpha* and *beta* are its first two. Their sense of self empowered them, too. They developed the idea that gods were like humans, and that humans could be like gods. In time, that democratized when they recognized that it is not kings and warriors, at the top of the social hierarchy, who are closest to the heavens but otherwise inconsequential individuals. What mattered was the quality of a person's soul, the radiance of their life. Hence, the cultivation of the individual became a key task. A person could aspire to know themselves and know the divine.

Perhaps the most striking parallel is that the Greeks also underwent a distinct period of inner transformation that left original participation behind. It began a couple of centuries after the reforms of the Deuteronomists and was ripe for synthesizing with the Jewish awareness of things by the time of Alexander the Great. It was similarly far-reaching and remarkable.

* * *

In his classic work, *The Story of Art*, E.H. Gombrich devotes an entire chapter to Greek art of the seventh to fifth centuries BCE. He calls this relatively short period, "The Great Awakening," and it's apt. In it, Greek culture visibly makes its equivalent of the Hebrew's inward, psychological turn. The artifacts of the era appear to wake up.

Before the awakening, art was decorated in what's known as the "geometric style" because it's characterized by regular patterns. The surviving pottery is adorned with repetitive designs that create an impression of liveliness but also conformity. When it comes to depicting human figures, the people-shaped silhouettes on the earliest pots have bull-like thighs, wasp-like waists, barrel-like chests, pin-like heads. The earliest Greek sculptures of humans are similarly distorted, at least so it seems to us, raising the question of what is going on with these apparently odd representations?

After all, the ancient Greeks clearly had bodies like ours. They must have differed in their sizes and proportions, heights and profiles as we do. And yet, any such naturalism is absent from the earliest art, and individual differences are ignored, too. The details that so interest us about human personhood seem not to have struck the artists and artisans of the geometric period.

The reason, Barfield and others have proposed, is that before the seventh century they did not experience themselves as individuals in the way that we do. The art accurately depicts how they did experience themselves: as facets of a collective. That collectivity reached into their internal self-awareness because, the thesis adds, they did not know their bodies as integrated entities either, but rather as baggy gatherings of spirited factions. It's what the art displays.

The possibility is supported by reading Homer. When a character of his era, like Achilles or Hector, reflects or feels, Homer describes the experience as isolated to specific parts of the body. It is not felt by the person as a whole. He'll talk of limbs being full of strength; of placing armor on the skin; of speedy knees. It's as if someone said, "My legs went for a run."

What we would think of as an inner life is equally dispersed. Important matters are debated with the lungs; talking is done by the belly; hearts are eased of sorrow. In fact, so dispersed were the forces inhabiting people, so fragmented was the vitality that animated them, that in the *Iliad* there is no word for a living body. The word that did come to mean the physical person, *soma*, refers only to corpses and remains, the empty flesh after its constellation of spirits has left. "Thus the Greeks [of this time] did not, either in their language or in the visual arts, grasp the body as a unit," summarizes Bruno Snell.[17]

This is the ancient Greek manifestation of original participation. The locus of aliveness wasn't set within a person's frame and physique. It wasn't inside that they felt their individuality. Instead, their identity came from the outside in, with different limbs and organs attuned to external divine influences. The inner life of the cosmos was their inner life. They had little or no notion of the isolated individual, like the early Israelites, and little sense of a unified self who was or could hope to be in charge. To be alive, to be functioning, was implicitly tied up with being porous to society, spirits, gods. This is the experience of life reflected in the iterations of patterned figures characteristic of the geometric style. The people appear to move as one, as if swaying in a field of consciousness like as many wheat ears blown by the wind.

It's this uniformity that changes when Greek art wakes up. It begins in the sixth century BCE. Take the statues of standing girls and youths, known as *korai* and *kouroi*. Before the change, Greek sculptors made these works along the same lines as the Assyrians and Egyptians, invariably following shared rules of sacred proportion. The distances between eyes and noses, nipples and belly-buttons don't change in statues that have been found as far apart as Greece's Delphi and Egypt's Memphis.

Then suddenly, the Greeks begin experimenting for themselves. They make knees look more realistic. They raise one foot, rather than having them both planted squarely on the ground. They put small turns into the corners of mouths looking a bit like smiles. As Gombrich remarks, from this moment onwards "every Greek sculptor wanted to know how *he* [sic] was to represent a particular body. The Egyptians had based their art on knowledge. The Greeks began to use their eyes."

The emphasis on the personal pronoun, *he*, carries massive significance. From the sixth century onwards, these artists were becoming individuals portraying individuals. They had started looking for themselves. They wanted to explore the idiosyncrasies of the human form, and capture what they found.

A particularly momentous occasion came when a painter of pots discovered the trick of foreshortening. He (presumably it was a man) painted a foot, but he did it as it would have looked from the front, not the traditional viewpoint that invariably showed feet lengthways, from the side. Five toes are drawn as a row of five circles. Technically, it's not hard to do and yet there is not a single surviving example of foreshortening in any work before. Gombrich dates the moment to a little before 500 BCE. The artist had become alert to the perspective from which he was viewing his subject. He had a point of view. It must have arisen from within him, as a result of a different sense of himself. These artists were no longer replicating images like state scribes but instead were gazing on the world around them. Life was beginning to be felt as springing from the inside-out as well as the outside-in. It's a massive extension of consciousness.

The Greek aristocracy tended to regard artists as inferiors, even when they showed such remarkable innovation. Perhaps it disturbed them, sensing that the move to what we call classical art was subtly disturbing the status quo. It was. Athenian democracy arose at the same time, presumably as part of the individualizing shift of mindset. It began to afford artists of genius public recognition and a few started to be remembered by name.

When the Acropolis was rebuilt after being sacked by the Persians in 480 BCE, Pericles asked the architect Iktinos and the sculptor Pheidias to work on the new temples. Pheidias, in particular, was a master of the awakening. His figures weren't generic presences with blank eyes. They looked at you. They conveyed a sense of alertness and interiority quite as vividly as Leonardo's Mona Lisa. His works were immediately recognized as spell-binding, displaying a dignity and beauty that called forth an interiority from within the viewer. He had captured and catalyzed a new conception of the human and divine, as well as the threshold between the two domains. His work was instrumental in showing a clear image of the integrated person, thereby spreading a sense of it in others.

A famous surviving example is the sculpture known as

the discus thrower of Myron. The athlete is just about to hurl the discus with agility and might, but the work is so striking because the balanced body also conveys the focus of the athlete's mind. You can feel his mental poise. Then, in the fourth century BCE, Praxiteles made a female nude known as the Aphrodite of Knidos. It displayed such breathtaking naturalism that an enamored sailor one day ensured he was locked up with the figure overnight. The story goes that he left semen stains on the paintwork when he departed in the morning.

In just over a century, a revolution had taken place. Preserved in the great works of the period, it was fired by a spark ignited within the great souls of the age – those who could detect an alternative to original participation. From then on, sculptors and painters who made the likenesses of groups of individuals learnt to portray the dynamics of interpersonal intercourse, capturing the sound of spoken words in stone and clay. The best sculptures could now show the workings and energies of the soul. They crafted the interactions of individuals. They left behind the collective swaying of the masses.

* * *

A parallel evolution of consciousness unfolded in the theater. Poetry before then had played an enormous role in public life. But again, it had been stylized, often formulaic. It was taught so as to confirm received opinions and propagate civic virtues. The work of a few, like Homer or Hesiod, is great but it lives without the concerns of ordinary people, instead focusing on tremendous forces, heroes and gods who pulse across battlefields and the cosmos. In their wake, mere mortals can only bob up and down. That's what life must have felt like. As Roberto Colasso explains: "Whenever their lives were set aflame, through desire or suffering, or even reflection, the Homeric heroes knew that a god was at work."[18] Their strength came from the outside in.

Then, in the sixth century BCE, personalities such as Alcaeus and Sappho started to appear as the authors of literature. They discovered that words can give form to private feelings. Sappho, for instance, describes her experiences of love. "It is as if my tongue is broken and immediately a subtle fire has run over my skin," murmurs fragment 31. The shift was taken up by the dramatists of the fifth century who pinpointed a similarly new locus of activity. It came from within themselves.

How that developed can be tracked across the works of the best tragedians of the time, the first being Aeschylus. Take his trilogy, the *Oresteia* of 458 BCE. It tells of what happened following the return of Agamemnon from the Trojan War and how the duty to avenge murder passes down the lines of the children and the children's children. It depicts the ramifications of blood feuds and, in many respects, feels like part of original participation. The knock-on effects of revenge reach to the third and fourth generation. Those who are caught up in this flow of violence have little choice but to participate in it. They are not so much individuals as noble or ignoble pawns, their virtue assessed by the manner in which they embrace their destiny. The gods are experienced as an irresistible fate, directing every part of the individual, even their hands and feet.

Similarly, the gods appear alongside the mortal characters, as if the divine and the human seamlessly mingle. Deities speak in the climatic moments of the drama to determine the outcome of lives. This is presumably how it felt and part of the thrill of Aeschylus's work when seen today comes from entering this, to us, alien environment. You feel its difference when the chorus offers warnings and laments in a single, unison voice. Pride and blood can't be questioned or resisted. The overall experience is emotionally intense as events sweep over the actors like a tsunami, caused by powers outside and above.

Things come a bit more down to earth with Sophocles, who inherited the role of leading playwright when Aeschylus died in 456 BCE. In his world, fate still inevitably unfolds but the characters he portrays are able to establish a degree of personal dignity. There is some sense of their inner lives. I think this is why Sophocles's plays contain sentiments that feel more like they could be our own. "All men make mistakes." "Reason is God's crowning gift to man." "In a just cause, the weak will beat the strong." He highlights features of an emerging experience of life that includes a role for individuals who can make mistakes, deploy reason, hold to virtues.

His best known work, *Oedipus Rex,* tells the story of Oedipus and how he unwittingly kills his father and has children by his mother. An oracle said he would and so he does. Oedipus is a king, a collective figure. These are qualities of original participation but Sophocles also conveys his pain in a way that feels more intimate. We can imagine him as an ordinary man, too. The play is a bit more biographical, you might say, a sense that develops in a later work, *Oedipus at Colonus*. Here, the former king, now a lost and wounded old man, relearns how to engage with life. Free of the oracle, and comforted by his children, he dies redeemed. He has struggled to shape his destiny and so made a place for his humanity in a cosmos not totally dominated by gods.

With the third dramatist of the century, Euripides, that trend deepens and becomes established. Euripides directly asks questions of life and the gods to the extent that it's often remarked that he is a "man of his times," a phrase that would have made no sense to use of anyone before. He consciously echoes the everyday uncertainties and challenges of his fellow Athenians, as well as grappling with the ramifications of their uneasy democracy. His tragedies are poignantly human, as in *The Trojan Women* that develops a female take on the horrors of war, or in *Medea* as the wife of Jason battles with her loss of power at the level of the personal and domestic, not divine and collective. Euripides writes for her a "proto-feminist speech in which she rails against the destiny of women," observes critic Jacqueline Rose. She cries out that women are "the most beset by trials of any species that has breath and power and thought."[19] That's new.

One of the most distinctive of Euripides's experiments is with the notion of conscience. With original participation, there is no conscience, no guilty party, but instead a terrible shame that ruins everyone involved. It's called a miasma. It's the same shared experience that's embedded in the older parts of the Hebrew Scriptures, where it entirely makes sense that punishment is shared. Moral pollution is caught like a plague and infected cities require general purification. Punishment is required after a wrongful action even if the perpetrator had no awareness of what they had done at all. There is no concept of a mistake, no issue of motive, which to us lies at the heart of justice. Those considerations are absent because there is not, as yet, the type of consciousness to arouse them. There was no individual.

But Euripides is one of the figures in the fifth century who develops a sense of buffered interiority and, with it, the individual is born and conscience is placed firmly on the moral agenda. As he puts it: clean hands are not the only issue. The heart must be clean, too.

He conveys the moment of transition in his play, *Hippolytus*. At one point, Phaedra, the wife of Theseus and secret lover of his son, Hippolytus, talks of the impure thoughts and disconcerting emotions boiling inside her, but her nurse takes her to be referring to magical attacks on her person. Phaedra must, therefore, suffer a private agony, in part because she cannot share her conscience with those who regard her predicament as an unfortunate curse to be cured by spells and charms.

Conscience isn't Euripides's invention. It's more like a discovery he makes, a glimpse of interiority that he catches, and there are indicators it was simultaneously emerging elsewhere.

Take the inscription at the temple of Asclepius in Epidaurus. It appears deliberately to redefine the notion of purity: "He who goes inside the sweet smelling temple must be pure. Purity is to think pious thoughts." There is the shift: purity as pious thoughts, not ritual cleanliness. For those who first read that, having just washed themselves or offered a sacrifice, the idea must have been confusing. It must have felt as disconcerting as the innovation of reading scripture rather than go to the temple, of being buried alone not in the clan grave.

Phaedra's love proves tragic. Individuality brings a rich array of pains, though Euripides realized that interiority has a distinctive advantage over original participation. It can offer consolation, an existential shield against the slings and arrows of the outrageous gods of fortune. "There is one thing alone that stands the brunt of life throughout its course: a quiet conscience," he writes. The reason is that the deities that exist all around, with the power to attack on a whim, are now not quite so omnipotent. The individual can mitigate things by an inner power of will. That's the gain. Shakespeare was later tellingly to call conscience, "this deity in my bosom."

* * *

Another development through the sixth and fifth centuries illuminates the Greek awakening from a third perspective. A group of individuals, now known as the philosophers, began to relate differently to the world around them. Their focus was the natural world and people's experience of it, and they sought to tease out a new understanding that could be called proto-scientific.

They launched debates about whether the cosmos is basically made of vital qualities they named water or fire or air or another ill-defined substance. In time, one of them, Anaxagoras, went so far as to propose that the Sun and the Moon may not be gods but that the Sun could be a fiery mass, perhaps of gold, and the Moon a place like the Earth. He added that they might be propelled across the heavens not by their own powers but by a unifying divine thought. If he were right that would mean that these celestial bodies weren't just to be related to, as seemed clear under original participation, but that they might also be understood. It's another manifestation of the withdrawal of participation, a kind of iconoclasm: honoring their influence and standing under them is supplemented with, and potentially eclipsed by, studying their qualities.

The philosophers began to conceive of their task as scrutinizing the world so as to glean knowledge. Thales of Miletus is said to have put his data to the test. One year he forecast that the next year's weather would be perfect for olives. Trusting his calculations, he borrowed money and bought all the olive presses in the region so that they had to be hired back from him. He duly made a fortune. Not that he was interested in money, he insisted, but rather in demonstrating the power of the new approach. It was very different from navigating nature's dynamics via myths. That had been about reading the runes of life not determining abstract cosmic principles.

Anaximenes was another philosopher who lived in Miletus. He was possibly taught by Thales and is remembered for another innovation: performing experiments. A record of one of his tests has survived the intervening centuries. He blew on one hand in two ways. First with his lips pursed: a puff. Then with his mouth open: a sigh. He noticed something. Or rather, he noticed something that presumably countless individuals before had noticed, only Anaximenes thought to think about what he noticed. When his lips were pursed, his breath felt cool to the hand. When his mouth was open, the air felt warm. And then he thought, why? It was his groundbreaking moment. He presumably shared the same experiences as his fellows and yet had now asked that small, awkward question.

He wasn't alone. Pythagoras is said to have walked past a blacksmith and noticed that when the blacksmith halved a bar of metal and hit it again, the note that sounded leapt a rather beautiful interval: an octave. It was an apparently unremarkable, humdrum sound. But Pythagoras noticed it, asked why, and it became remarkable. He sparked epoch-defining inquiries into the links between mathematics, nature and beauty. Eventually, it shaped the scientific revolution, and the time when Galileo could remark that we're all Pythagoreans now.

Anaximenes came up with an answer to his question about breath. Today, it's taught as Boyle's Law. When air expands, as breath does when forced through lips that are pursed, it cools. It's the science behind fridges and air conditioners. Except, its subsequent technological application in the modern world is not what marked out Anaximenes's experiment at first. He wasn't immediately celebrated as a scientist but, along with Pythagoras and others, for discovering the quality of mind upon which such investigations rest. His contribution to the Greek revolution was, again, an awakening. He helped shift the experience of what it is to be human.

He thought about the inside of the experiment. He noticed that there could be a mental space between the experience and thinking about the experience, and that gap proved crucial. What the sculptors had shown in the astonishing gaze of their figures, and the playwrights had portrayed in the stresses of their characters, the philosophers were unpacking in the abstractions of thought. They were developing a capacity of mind that could take a step back. It implies a sense of yourself that is separate from what's going on and, springing from that, comes a feeling of inner and outer; me and not me; immanence and transcendence.

It's a brave new world of interiority because an "I" forms in conjunction with the question "why." I suspect that's why, today, young children go through a phase of repeatedly asking it. They're not just intrigued by the word. They're intrigued about the power within themselves to keep on asking. "I" can sit a bit apart from the immersive flow of stuff happening. Someone who can say "I am" can occupy a place of stillness to consider things. There's a separation, a momentary uncoupling, a pause. There's the individual's interior castle and then there's the rest of the world. It's a refuge unknown in a mythical world and is gained from a withdrawal of participation.

It can also be disturbing. To ask why is to risk the experience of doubt, uncertainty, perhaps panic because if an individual has withdrawn once from the flow of nature, they can do so again and again. Eventually, it might be hard to know how to step back. It's for this reason that, with the first philosophers, the meaning of life becomes an issue for the first time in human history. They found themselves confronted by a question that hadn't occurred to Homer, for whom the meaning of life was a non-question. He was confronted by an overflow of meaning, with the gods pressing in. His issue was how that flood might be negotiated. It's why we think of philosophy beginning during this time. The questions formulated then are still ours now. Like the Deuteronomists, the Greek philosophers were the midwives to our consciousness of life.

They could get into trouble for giving it voice. Pythagoras is said to have been persecuted wherever he traveled. He gathered groups of followers who lived peripatetic lives. They were held together not by loyalty to clan or place, but by their quest and way of life. Much as wanderers today stir up feelings of suspicion and insecurity, so the Pythagoreans became targets. Pythagoras himself was said to have been murdered by his opponents.

The tension came to a head in about the year 432 BCE, when the Athenian state acted against what it regarded as the philosophers' sacrilegious, anarchic teaching. They were lumped together as "atheists," a word that at the time meant believing in the gods in the wrong way, rather than not believing in gods at all. The Sun should not be downgraded to gold, as

Anaxagoras had speculated. The received wisdom about deities should not be doubted, as another of their number, Protagoras, had wondered. "The next thirty-odd years witnessed a series of heresy trials which is unique in Athenian history," reports E.R. Dodds.[20] Alongside Anaxagoras and Protagoras, others including Euripides and Socrates were prosecuted. They were accused of treason which, under original participation, is indistinguishable from idolatry and faithlessness because gods were the life of the people.

Philosophers were banished, others fled, a handful died. It's possible that books were publicly burned. Plato later remarked that the life of a philosopher exposes them to ill-will and conspiracy "so that most of them find it necessary to work undercover." They were not unlike the prophets in this regard.

They were similar in another way. Much as the biblical authors insisted that idols have eyes but see not, some philosophers deployed that rhetoric. There's Heraclitus, another key thinker of the age. He remarked that "a person's character is their fate," a truly astonishing proposition when most people must have still felt mightily pushed around by forces from above. He also noted how people "pray to statues of gods who do not hear them as though they heard them," and then took the observation a further step. He began to formulate the possibility that nature was not governed by a pantheon of gods, who ruled from this mountain and that dell, but rather by a universal principle that runs uniformly through the whole of nature. He called it the *Logos*. He was implying that the location of nature's dynamism is not sacred places. Rather, if you learn to direct your attention aright, you'll see that sacred places and divine objects transmit a source of life that transcends them. It is a perception that was to have a long history, as any reader of the opening verse of John's gospel will realize: "In the beginning was the Word," or *Logos*. For Heraclitus, this was not yet experienced as the sustaining aspect of a monotheistic God, as Christians were to conclude.

Nonetheless, he articulated a clear sense that whilst divinity can be experienced immanently in nature, the divine itself must originate in a realm that is outside of nature. It is nature's wellspring and sustainer, not only its spirit. This is why it's a mistake to worship statues of gods, or the Sun and the Moon. It's not *their* influence that is beaming on us. Instead, celestial bodies should be thought of as reflecting a vigor that lies above and beyond all things. Plato, for example, came to call the Sun "the offspring of the Good."

Heraclitus felt it right to describe the *Logos* as a fiery force, one that fills the cosmos with an order that marries stability and flux. He argued that the *Logos* is everlasting. "Listening not to me but to the *Logos*, it is wise to agree that all things are one," advises another surviving fragment of his sayings. He was also clear that what he had detected of the *Logos* far outstrips the power of human minds fully to understand. "Of this account, which holds forever, men prove uncomprehending," is another remark, underlining the perception of transcendence.

There's a story that a book by Heraclitus was given to Socrates by Euripides. The playwright subsequently asked the philosopher what he made of it. "What I understand is splendid," Socrates replied, "And so too, I'm sure, is what I don't. But it would take a Delian diver to get to the bottom of it."

* * *

Like the deep sea divers from Delos, the philosophers quickly realized that plunging into the depths of things requires rigorous training. The individual becomes wise only if they first work on themselves, in the sense of reflecting on the type of self they possess. If that went well, they might become attuned and able consciously to participate in the cosmos around them, resonating like an antenna. Their inner life might become a receiver of knowledge. The sage was someone who had the capacity to catch different levels of reality and speak about what they saw. As with the discovery of monotheism, and the need for an "I am" that could mirror the "I AM," their project involved the personality as much as powers of cognition.

It invited followers to form a psychic bond with the cosmos, to reconnect after the withdrawal, only this time in a deliberate way. The philosophers strove consciously to know of something by sharing in its being, rather than just tacitly to know about something, as the myths had allowed. But it was demanding. Coming to know things in the fuller sense is a question of you and your way of life. It's not a detached investigatory activity. Only the beautiful soul can contemplate what's beautiful because the two then chime together. Only the well-ordered psyche can discern the orders of nature, because if the psyche is disordered it will be preoccupied with its shadows. Only the lover of excellence can glimpse the excellence of what's changeless because love's yearning, gradually, orientates such an individual towards it. Much as the Sun is a child of the Good, so a person's intelligence might become akin to the intelligence of the cosmos.

What this knowledge is like can be seen by considering Anaximenes again. It seems that he didn't just ask why the pressured air feels cooler and the "slack" air stays warm, as a physicist might do today, and be satisfied when an adequate explanation is settled. His observation led him to ponder about the relationship between hot and cold, and what that might mean about life. He wanted to get back on the inside of what he'd observed not just linger, looking on. What remains of his work is scant but my sense is that he might have continued his speculations along these lines.

First, he might have noted, the relationship between hot and cold is not one of opposites. You can catch a glimpse of the disparity in the words themselves because whereas it somehow makes sense to say, "cold is a lack of heat," it doesn't make sense to say, "heat is a lack of cold." Heat is real. Back then, they'd have said it's spirit; today we say it's energy. But coldness is different. It is an absence of heat, a lack of energy, an emptiness.

This could have led to a further reflection. Air is clearly linked to life, and further, it's warm air that is linked to life because when creatures die, warm breath leaves their bodies, which then grow cold. So perhaps life and death have an asymmetric relationship that mirrors hot and cold. Death is an absence of life, in a way that life isn't an absence of death. Perhaps, further again, this is an intimation that life is prior to death, it contains death, and can't be extinguished by death.

It isn't just a question of reason, but of felt experience. A key component, Plato explains picking up Anaximenes's intuitive logic, is becoming appropriately attached to physical life. That was something he knew about having been a wrestler before meeting Socrates. He was good enough to compete in the Isthmian Games, history records, the warm-up to the ancient Olympics, and was trained by the noted Ariston of Argon. His name, Plato, was actually a pen name, being a pun on the Greek for "broad," as in broad-shouldered. His real name was Aristocles. So, Plato, "Mr Physical," was drawn to perceiving the ways in which the trained body radiates with a life that exceeds its physicality alone. Plato referred to that excessiveness as the soul. The soul is the life that emanates from the body, much as music is the sound that emerges from the lyre. You need a body to be aware of more than the body, you might say – at least that's the case for us mortals. Such possibilities had become thinkable and could be subtly felt.

It could be detected in nature and the cosmos, too, as Plato explored in his visionary dialogue, the *Timaeus*. Here, he likens the created universe to the work of the demiurge, an imagined divine craftsman. The dialogue seeks to portray the extraordinary intricacy and patterning of this fictitious god's genius workmanship. These days, it's more helpful to think of the demiurge as a divine musician than a divine craftsman because, since the scientific revolution, the craft metaphor has become loaded with images of mechanics and engineering. It's hard not to think of the demiurge as an intelligent watchmaker who spends his long days tweaking the dials of the cosmic clock. But Plato's original intention was to draw on more organic analogies, such as are found in song and music. A composer keeps an eye on notes, tunes and harmonies. Plato's cosmic "musician" strives to make a magnificent idea heard, and judges what is produced by its overall effects and excellences. The philosopher, too, might hear this music of the spheres with a well-tuned inner ear.

Plato had a verb for it: "immortalling." Today, we might call it contemplating – the art of channeling what's more than this world into this world. It's a task the philosopher could aspire to because of the richness of the interiority he or she felt opening up inside them. Aristotle, Plato's greatest pupil, put it like this: "We must not heed those who advise us to think as human beings since we are human and to think mortal things since we are mortal, but we must be like immortals insofar as possible and do everything toward living in accordance with the best thing in us" (*Nicomachean Ethics*, 1177b). And there was one person they agreed had achieved this: Socrates.

Chapter 4

The Athenian Moses

The figure that the philosophers came to hang the new consciousness on was Socrates. Like the Deuteronomists's Moses, he became the exemplary teacher and prophet, in the sense of being the herald of what was humanly possible. He was the philosophers's transitional object, the one through whom they worked out how high human beings might reach, how deep they might dive.

Born in the middle of the fifth century BCE, an almost exact contemporary of Euripides, he thoroughly embraced the philosophers' revolution and brought things into focus, not through sculpture, though he had trained as a mason, and not through writing, which he perhaps couldn't do, but in his own person. The hallmark of his mature philosophy was developing a supreme care for the soul. That care must be nurtured in the midst of the everyday, so he taught in the heart of Athens, the marketplace, where he walked and talked.

He felt he had a calling from Apollo and had received sanction from Apollo's oracle at Delphi. The god drew him for a number of reasons, one of which is embedded in the name. A-pollo means "not many," as, conversely, *hoi polloi* means "the many." Apollo was the Greek god of the emerging, gathered I-consciousness, and focusing on this deity, who was one, could help integrate the person and reveal the underlying unity of things. The Neoplatonists of the first centuries CE were to rename Apollo, the One, which some Jews and Christians recognized as the same as the one God.

Socrates talked about his experience of the divine indirectly, often in relation to his daemon. "I have a divine or spiritual sign," he testifies in Plato's dialogue, the *Apology*. "This began when I was a child" (*Apology*, 31d). It was not a malign spirit, as the word demon was to come to imply. At the time of Socrates, daemons were simply go-between spirits who mediated mortal and immortal forces. They could be angels. For example, Plato wrote of Eros, one of the gods of love, as a daemon with remarkable, attractive powers.

Socrates's daemon could be described as a striking experience of conscience. It was the deity in his bosom. "It is something like a voice," he explained. However, it was an inner voice with a particular intention, one working with the spirit of the age. For as Socrates continues: "Whenever it speaks it turns me away from something I am about to do, but it never encourages me to do anything."

It followed a negative way. It did not command or cajole Socrates, let alone work him like a puppet, as Homer's characters had experienced the gods' impingements and intrusions. Instead, by advising, though without straightforward instruction, it put the onus back on Socrates. He had to work at what might be revealed, a revelation that could only become clear when located in his heart and mind. You could say that the truth was disclosed slowly. It's a bit like devotional reading. It was prompted by Apollo, stirred up by the go-between, realized in Socrates. Socrates's daemon wasn't just telling him what to do, it was inviting him to participate in the truth. In so doing, he became more of an individual. His soul grew as he was invited to share in the life of the gods. He could be their co-worker.

Sometimes the daemon seized on seemingly trivial things, like not rising from his seat as he was about to leave the palaestra. On this occasion, he reports that he didn't, and a remarkably fruitful conversation ensued with individuals who subsequently arrived. At other times, working with his inner voice was more challenging, as when it advised him not to become involved in public life, which he took to mean that he was called to pursue a distinctive, individual vocation. That bred suspicion about his intentions, and culminated in his trial. The daemon had a comment about that too: don't resist it. He could trust what unfolded, even though his accusers were corrupt; even if the process led to his death, which it did. He was glad to cooperate with Apollo because he had learnt that, in ways he didn't wholly understand, Apollo would only point him towards what is good – a goodness that became part of his character. It shone through him, for those who had eyes to see. As Phaedo averred to a friend, as he recalled witnessing Socrates die: "That man was the best" (*Phaedo*, 118a).

That happened in 399 BCE, when Socrates was found guilty in one of the heresy trials, imprisoned and condemned to drink hemlock. The generations of philosophers who followed realized the city had made a terrible mistake. They worried that in killing their greatest son, Athens jeopardized the humanity that had made it great. The death of Socrates sparked a welter of writing that tried to remember, convey and learn from the spirit of the man. It reached its greatest expression in the writing of Plato.

* * *

He took a lead from how Socrates had described his negative way that is captured in the Greek word, *aporia*. It means "without resource," or being at your wits' end. He had been captivated by the potential of his own troubling encounter with Socrates and, in response, developed a training for others that might replicate it in them. That became the basis for the school he set up in Athens, the Academy. The training centered on tolerating this state of unknowing, the gap of meaning with which humanity must, he felt, learn to live because if that can be achieved, the gap morphs into a receptacle. It becomes the means of receiving intimations of the eternal, of the soul, of nature, the heavens and the gods. It's what Anaximenes had intuited and Socrates had realized.

A sense of this process can be gained by thinking about how poetry works. The power of the poetic is that it discloses and points beyond itself, a process that can parallel the philosopher's moments of *aporia*. Both forms can bring the individual to a threshold, from which they are able to look beyond the immediate.

It doesn't always work like this in poetry, of course. Consider "Up-Hill" by Christina Rossetti.[21] The first verse reads:

Does the road wind up-hill all the way?
Yes, to the very end.
Will the day's journey take the whole long day?
From morn to night, my friend.

The poem continues in a similar vein and does not take its reader to any edge of knowing because it is clear throughout what the poet is talking about. An arduous journey. It achieves another goal, that of illuminating a clearly defined experience.

It's very different in the case of "The Listeners" by Walter de la Mare.[22] The poem also describes a journey, but picks things up at the end of the traveler's labors and, at first, it seems aimed at describing the experience, too.

'Is there anybody there?' said the Traveller,
Knocking on the moonlit door;
And his horse in the silence champed the grasses
Of the forest's ferny floor.

But then it becomes clear that the journey of the traveler is only the surface interest of the poet. Another reality is hiding itself within the poem. The reader is brought to an edge as they strive to glimpse it.

And he smote upon the door again a second time;

'Is there anybody there?' he said.
But no one descended to the Traveller;
No head from the leaf-fringed sill
Leaned over and looked into his grey eyes,
Where he stood perplexed and still.
But only a host of phantom listeners
That dwelt in the lone house then
Stood listening in the quiet of the moonlight
To that voice from the world of men.

De la Mare continues, highlighting the "strangeness" of these listeners from another world. They are known by their stillness, shadowiness, silence, and they are disturbing, leaving the traveler feeling he hasn't the resources to comprehend them.

For he suddenly smote on the door, even
Louder, and lifted his head:—
'Tell them I came, and no one answered,
That I kept my word,' he said.

The reader is left wondering about that promise and to what reality it is made. It's the same sense of the implicit that Plato felt Socrates was pointing to with his questions and that brought him to his wits' end. Although, on the other side of the discomfort, lay the promise of an entirely different sight: a sense of the inside of things with which he might partake.

That fullness is caught in a third poem, by Andrew Marvell, a poet who is overtly Platonic. "The Garden" again begins by celebrating something tangible, in this case the visible joys of nature:

What wond'rous life in this I lead!
Ripe apples drop about my head;
The luscious clusters of the vine

Upon my mouth do crush their wine;
The nectarine and curious peach
Into my hands themselves do reach;
Stumbling on melons as I pass,
Ensnar'd with flow'rs, I fall on grass.

But this "wond'rous life," with its "curious peach," becomes a bridge across which the poet approaches an unveiling. He discovers the invisible, subtle pleasures that are found not in the garden but through it, in the garden of the mind. They are found to be even more wonderful. They are transcendent, uncreated, divine.

Meanwhile the mind, from pleasure less,
Withdraws into its happiness;
The mind, that ocean where each kind
Does straight its own resemblance find,
Yet it creates, transcending these,
Far other worlds, and other seas;
Annihilating all that's made
To a green thought in a green shade.

Then, in the next verse, the poet brings the two realities together. He realizes that "far other worlds" are detectable only because the luscious world of the garden awoke him to them. The garden, like the embodied world in general, can shine with a life that is more than its own. It's like the sound of the music of the spheres. Marvell, following Plato, realized that this world can be loved not only for its own sake but because of the spiritual reality with which it communes and is joined. In Marvell's words:

Here at the fountain's sliding foot,
Or at some fruit tree's mossy root,
Casting the body's vest aside,

My soul into the boughs does glide;
There like a bird it sits and sings,
Then whets, and combs its silver wings;
And, till prepar'd for longer flight,
Waves in its plumes the various light ...

* * *

Greek philosophers, like the Deuteronomic Jews, launched the development of a reciprocal participation. In contrast to the immersion of original participation, and the alienation of withdrawn participation, a reciprocal consciousness experiences its life as if it were a mirror reflecting more. A Socratic training was, therefore, akin to polishing the reflective surface of the mind. The truer it became, the more light it gathered and the more it might reflect what is good, beautiful and true. "As within, so without" became the Christian summary of this way.

Practically speaking, it involved contemplating the inner nature of everyday things, like friendship or courage or justice. Plato shows how Socrates asked all his questions not so as to find definitions, as if in pursuit of a decent entry for a dictionary. Rather, the aim is consciously to explore what might open up when the multiple facets of something are meditated upon. His 30-odd dialogues take the task on. They work not by telling the reader what to think but by inviting the reader to reflect on the twists and turns of experience, understanding that it is the act of wondering itself that creates the gap into which illumination can flow. It is like a lightening flash brightening the darkness, he writes in the so-called *Seventh Letter*, that opens not the physical eye but the eye of the soul.

Consider, one of his dialogues on love, the human experience that preoccupied Plato the most. The *Phaedrus* is set by a river, which Plato spends several pages detailing. The river is the Ilisus, Socrates explains to the eponymous Phaedrus, the young man with whom he is walking in the dialogue. It's the home of the river god, Achelous, the sage adds.

Invoking the divine names makes the two of them aware of the hidden presence. It creates a seductive mood that allows Socrates to point to what might be beyond: "Feel the freshness of the air; how pretty and pleasant it is; how it echoes with the summery, sweet song of the cicadas's chorus!" he exclaims. It's mesmerizing, but by becoming conscious of the enchantment, he can take advantage of the surroundings to begin a discussion about love.

The river and its deities provide a perfect setting because, on the bankside, beneath the dappled light of the trees, the links made by love can be felt. The links between self and other, spirit and matter, reason and passion, human and divine reveal themselves. Socrates and Phaedrus have the opportunity not just to talk about, but to know of, this psychopomp. Socrates's goal is to cultivate Phaedrus's awareness of it. He brings the energies without and the thought within into harmonic alignment. Together, the friends follow the delight they feel in their souls, and so attune to love.

* * *

It's not the way philosophy is usually approached these days. Now, it's often regarded, and taught, as a dry, abstract subject which deliberately aims to quench the flames of experience. In order to reclaim Plato's inner music, it's necessary to think carefully about the key words the ancient philosophers used so as to regain a sense of what his earlier reciprocal consciousness was driving at.

One would be the word *logos,* and its derivatives. These are often translated as "word" or "reason" or "arguments." But, as Barfield writes, "Reason is quite inadequate to convey to a twentieth-century imagination the cosmic process which Plato must have felt to be taking place – as much out in the world and among the stars as 'within' his own mind."[23] That's one reason why the *Logos* was such a crucial realization.

Similarly, *nous* is often translated as "mind" or "intellect," words that easily erase what Plato evoked. For him, *nous* is a receptive capacity, a seat of awareness, as much associated with the heart as the head. It's why love is such an essential capacity for the philosopher because philosophy is about feeling as well as thinking. *Nous* responds as much to beauty as logic. "Poetry is the cradle of philosophy," averred John of Salisbury in this spirit. The training that Plato designed similarly incorporated an education in mathematics, dialectic and reason in order to develop the commensurate facilities of analogy, intuition and discernment. With that, you could learn of the relationship between life and death by contemplating the relationship between hot and cold.

Barfield went so far as to advise that, nowadays, it is better at first to assume you've not understood what Plato meant by such words. Modern thought will probably have changed the meaning so radically that the first task is to "unthink" what you know.

> [A modern European] can read Plato and Aristotle through from end to end, he can even write books expounding their philosophy, and all without understanding a single sentence. Unless he has enough imagination, and enough power of detachment from the established meanings or thought-forms of his own civilization, to enable him to grasp the meanings of the fundamental terms – unless, in fact, he has the power not only of thinking, but of *unthinking* – he will simply re-interpret everything they say in terms of subsequent thought.[24]

It is not just a question of translating words, Barfield continues, but of feeling "the way in which they *came into being*." Plato treated words as if they might unveil reality. Their secret life could bring felt qualities to awareness. He, too, was a poet, and became very exercised when other poets squandered their gift.

Consider how he taught numbers. They are interesting and useful, he felt, but not primarily because of how they can be used to add things up. At the time, there was, in fact, no word for "quantity." This notion hadn't yet been fully forged. Instead, numbers were important because of the qualities they convey. It's their secret life. Contemplating "oneness" is more important than nailing what "1" measures. What is it to be one, unity, singular? How does that differ from what's two, dual, divided?

Plato describes how, one day, Socrates became fascinated by watching two raindrops fall together, collide, and merge to form one raindrop. It must have been a beautiful thing to observe, but it also peaked his curiosity. Where did the twoness go?

It's in this sense that philosophically-inspired Christian theologians became fascinated by the quality of threeness in relation to perceiving God as three persons in one. "Whoever can conceive of distinction without quantity, knows that three Persons are a single God," observed Meister Eckhart, before continuing: "If there were a hundred Persons in the Godhead, they would see only one God. Unbelievers and some uneducated Christians are astounded at this, even some priests know as little about it as a stone does, and take three in the sense of three cows or three stones."[25] Threeness is robust like a tripod; it's three-dimensional in its height, depth and breadth; it shows something fully expressed, as when Shakespeare declares a particularly evil person "thrice a villain" or someone calls for "Three Cheers!" Two would not be enough. Aristotle spelt it out: "The triad is the number of the complete whole, inasmuch as it contains a beginning, a middle, and an end" (*On the Heavens I.1*).

Plato was drawn to maths to contemplate how different numbers participate in various fundamental aspects, or forms, of being. It's mathematics as a perceptive practice. It directs the eye of the soul so as to reflect on the dynamics implicit on the inside of the world. Similarly, Plato's Academy became well known for its astronomical observations not because its members were enthusiasts for gathering stellar data, though they gathered lots. Rather, they felt that observing the heavens was a supreme way of polishing minds. That immediately makes sense when you take a moment to gaze and wonder at the immensity of the night sky and its numerous stars, and notice the stillness that settles inside. That's a quality of infinity. Seen in this light, the cosmos becomes a performance of the beauty of God.

It was also the meaning of the legendary sign that Plato had posted above the entrance to the Academy: "Let no one ignorant of geometry enter." It wasn't a ban so much as a statement. Anyone ignorant of the harmonies of geometry wouldn't be able to appreciate what Plato and the academicians were up to. They might think they had split analysis from analogy, thinking from feeling, body from soul.

This is also crucial when considering Plato's so-called "proofs." They are not logical proofs in the modern sense but are rather "explorations by analogy." They offer the kind of knowledge that's gained not by the accumulation of facts but by uniting them. It's like Anaximenes's exploration of the relationship between heat and cold, that points.

Plato used the same examples when he came to think about immortality by testing out the dynamics that are felt in nature. Do they not always come in pairs, Socrates invites his interlocutors to consider in the *Phaedo* – pairs of cooling and heating, of separating and combining? Can you feel that death may be no different, if it's part of a cycle too, of dying and living? The intuition is that death could include a return to life.

He's not offering an argument in the usual sense, and it completely misses the point to insist such a proposition is flawed and demonstrate where its logic falls apart. That forgets that analogies are indicative, not themselves what is being indicated. The mistake is a bit like the Zen disciple who becomes preoccupied with the finger of his master pointing at the Moon and so never follows the direction of travel.

Other key words remind us of sustaining the effort to unthink what we think we know. The word "speculation" is one. It comes from the Greek, *skeptomai*, meaning to look at or examine, which Latin speakers translated into *speculor*. The implication is that Plato didn't indulge in speculation in our sense, as in taking a punt on notions. That kind of speculation has financial overtones that only became associated with philosophical activity in the eighteenth century. Rather, Plato sought to see.

Similarly, "theory" did not mean a hypothesis but, originally, referred to a journey that was undertaken so as to experience a life-changing event. A *theoria* in Plato's day was not to be tested but was, rather, a kind of pilgrimage. The best known example Plato provides is that of the journey out of the cave, often referred to as the myth of the cave, in which he envisages prisoners held at the back of a deep grotto. They see shadows on the wall and take them for reality, until one of them manages to turn around and, after an immense individual effort, find a way to the mouth of the cave to be met by an astonishing sight. The light of the Sun, the child of the Good. Only then, after his journey, is the true nature of reality realized.

Another "theory" is the one that ends the *Republic*. It tells of how a man called Er had apparently been killed in a battle and was about to be cremated, when he awoke. He told his fellows that he had been on a journey to the land of the dead where he had witnessed how the living must account for themselves in the afterlife. Plato records Er's experience at great length, inviting us to go on the journey, too.

Aristotle picked up the baton from Plato, having studied with him for 26 years before Plato died, and himself coined several words that are worth unpicking. The neologisms capture his own response to the Socratic method – words like "analysis." It includes the stem "lysis," to break down, as in electrolysis, and shows how Aristotle sought to open up the nature of things by peering into their manifest appearances. He felt himself to be participating in what he studied because, for him, analysis arose when the mind turns towards the world and detects the dynamics, patterns and order it encounters there. His mind felt its way into his objects of study, teasing out the differences between the different species of plants or the categories to which things belonged. "Struggling to fit herself, as into a glove, to the processes of cause and effect observed in physical phenomena, the mind became suddenly conscious of her own shape. She was astonished and delighted," Barfield says, describing how Aristotle's philosophy works.[26] Aristotle's analysis complemented Plato's analogies. And they both follow their master, Socrates. Their philosophy was nothing if it didn't spring from caring for their souls.

* * *

At about this time came Alexander. He had as big an impact upon Greek philosophy as he did on ancient Judaism, doing more than any other to spread Greek thought and values.

He had asserted his rule in Athens five years before he entered Jerusalem, after the Greek city-state had sued for peace. The people had initially rebelled when Alexander assumed the throne. It had only recently been incorporated into the Macedonian empire and some Athenians read the moment as a chance to reclaim their democracy, mocking the young successor as an idiot. They misjudged the new king and, luckily for the Athenians, one of their number, Phocion, regained Alexander's confidence. It might also have helped that Alexander had been taught for a while by Aristotle.

The city quickly found itself at the cultural heart of the general's expanding empire. The new consciousness of the artists, the playwrights and the philosophers found a mode of global transport.

It had a profound effect upon the generation of philosophers that followed Plato and Aristotle. In particular, it intensified the individualizing trend. Whereas Pheidias, Euripides and Socrates had assumed that an individual's well-being, whilst pre-eminent, was intimately tied to the flourishing of the city-state, the Hellenistic schools tended to turn more exclusively inwards. They cultivated what Pierre Hadot has called "spiritual exercises."[27] These were practices of self-examination, self-awareness and self-expression that developed self-knowledge of personal errors and weaknesses, virtues and strengths. The aim was to secure an interior equanimity.

The exercises stressed the value of the present moment because, unlike the past and the future, it is the only moment over which the individual has any influence. The goal was to be able to affirm, "I have lived!" "Spiritual exercises almost always correspond to the movement by which the 'I' concentrates itself upon itself and discovers that it is not what it had thought," Hadot remarks.[28] They were refashioning the Socratic *aporia*. The Hellenistic philosopher was one whose conquests were directed inwards to win the mastery known by the sage: control of themselves. It was a novel goal, another step change in the evolution of consciousness.

A number of different philosophy schools emerged, sharing the goal, though offering various methods by which to achieve it. The Epicureans taught that the key is tolerating pain and developing a capacity to take pleasure in small things. "I am as happy as Zeus feasting on Mount Olympus, when all I have is a glass of water and a barley cake," is a surviving aphorism of their founder, Epicurus. With the steadiness of mind such an attitude safeguards, the Epicurean was then free to explore the hidden reaches of the cosmos. The Roman poet, Lucretius, describes it in his epic poem, *On the Nature of Things*, in which he salutes the genius of Epicurus: "The keen force of his mind conquered, and he advanced far beyond the blazing walls of the universe and traversed the immense whole with his mind and soul, whence, a conqueror, he brought back to us the account of what can arise and what cannot, and by what rational principle each thing has its power bounded."

The Cynics were different. They felt that what imprisons and limits human beings are the externalities of social conventions. People want to live in fine houses, eat the best food, dress fashionably, marry well, have money, be respectable. They will live their lives so as to impress others, rather than so as to be free in their souls. So they tried to live without the rules and customs that, they felt, are so restrictive. It shocked many, who said they were dogs, which in Greek is *kynikos*, or Cynic. The "dogs" adopted the name for their school.

Whilst never popular in terms of numbers, they were successful in terms of being long-lasting. Cynics could be heard begging and provoking others to embrace true freedom right through the Hellenistic and Roman periods. Here's how Hipparchia of Maroneia, the wife of Crates, put it: "I have never been fond of the brooch that fastens my garments, and neither have I been pleased with the bound foot and the headband daubed with perfume. But a staff, and bare feet and whatever folded cloak clings from my limbs, and the hard ground instead of a bed, these I have chosen."[29]

They were peripatetic philosophers, another sign of their individualism and rejection of social norms. In time, they were found wandering throughout the Mediterranean, preaching on street corners. The sight of an unkempt outsider, proclaiming antisocial messages, must have been strange. To not respect bonds of kinship and citizenship was still generally regarded as odd, if not treacherous. It's easy to imagine passersby crossing to the other side of the street. They developed an arresting form of communication, too, the diatribe. In one surviving example,

Teles of Megara, extols the virtues of poverty by imaging poverty addressing him. Poverty says: "Surely you don't lack for anything necessary? Are not the roadsides full of vegetables? Aren't the springs filled with water, and don't I provide you with a bed wherever there is earth, and a couch of leaves?"[30] Teles's aim wasn't to idealize poverty, but simply to persuade himself and others that his soul had little to fear from having nothing because social norms had nothing of real value to offer him to start with.

If the Cynics were influential, the most widespread of the schools in terms of numbers and reach was Stoicism. In time, it was to name statesmen amongst its adherents, not least in the second century CE, the Roman emperor, Marcus Aurelius. Stoics taught that the emotional flux of the human mind was the enemy within that might undo you. They cultivated a kind of self-centeredness: choosing what is good for you over what is bad, on the understanding that nothing is as good for you as taking care of your inner life; your soul. Again, prioritizing that would have seemed peculiar, perhaps incomprehensible before. It's why Stoics became associated with suicide in the popular imagination: these were the philosophers who preferred death and staying loyal to their values, over their lives and preserving themselves.

Their therapy fostered an inner capacity to step back from the ups and downs of the everyday, which led to a remarkable discovery. When less distracted by humdrum concerns, they found that the *Logos* of Heraclitus could be discerned pulsing through the sinews of things. "Dig within; for within you lies the fountain of good, and it can always be gushing forth if only you always dig," wrote Marcus. Seneca, another articulate Stoic, likened it to tilling the soil of the soul, with the careful individual playing the part of farmer. "Divine seeds are scattered throughout our mortal bodies; if a good husbandman receives them, they spring up in the likeness of their source and of a parity with those from which they came. If, however, the husbandman be bad, like a barren or marshy soil, he kills the seeds, and causes tares to grow up instead of wheat."

Another Stoic, Epictetus, was to emphasize the discovery even more: "You are a fragment of God; you have within you a part of Him. Why, then, are you ignorant of your own kinship? Why do you not know the source from which you have sprung? You are bearing God about with you, and know it not!"

These were tremendous claims, and although philosophy was a minority and relatively elite concern in Antiquity, it was not without impact. Recent research has documented about 2,500 surviving names of ancient philosophers, of whom about 85 are women. So, if philosophy were confined to the top 10 percent of the population, those with the leisure and literacy to pursue it, it was a significant social movement among the upper echelons. Then, less directly, it could reach down further.

Evidence for this includes an Epicurean inscription found engraved on a public wall, advertising the philosophy that will lead to personal salvation. Alternatively, Stoic sentiments are likely to have shaped the culture of extended families in those households that were headed up by an adherent. There's also what happened in 155 BCE. By this time, Athens was no longer under Macedonian rule because it had fallen to Rome. When Athens sacked the village of Oropos in that year, it was punished with a monumental fine imposed by the Roman Senate. The amount would have crippled Athens for decades so a decision was taken to appeal to the authorities, and to do so by sending an embassy of philosophers to Rome.

The group included the head of Plato's Academy, Carneades; the head of Aristotle's Lyceum, Critolaus; and the head of the Stoic school, Diogenes of Babylon. It was a cultural and diplomatic triumph. So impressive were the philosophers that the Senate ruled to settle the affair quickly in Athens's favor, though what may have stirred the Roman aristocracy was fear as much as admiration. They seem to have sensed that philosophy might inspire the youth of Rome away from traditional virtues. These norms were still focused not on newfangled worries about self-development but the older practices of civic consciousness, such as venerating clan ancestors and maintaining family honor. Philosophy still represented what appeared to some to be a dangerous wrench from original participation.

The senatorial conservatives were not mistaken in their concerns. Stoic philosophy particularly appealed to Romans. A couple more generations later, Cicero had prepared and published several summaries of its insights in Latin. He understood it thoroughly, from the inside, but it must have taken all his ingenuity to translate and popularize the Greek terms that had developed to express its dynamic and life. We use his terms still and routinely talk of "individuals" and "essences," "qualities" and "questions."

* * *

Philosophy was not the only Greek force opening up the secrets of the soul during this period. In the Hellenistic age, the old catharsis that had been found in the fifth-century plays of Sophocles and Euripides gradually migrated to the institutions called the mysteries. The ancient origins of these religious initiation rites are lost in time. For centuries they had existed as just one more ritual way of dealing with the impact of the gods on life. But their meaning now evolved. They became more personal and began to focus on self-knowledge.

Socrates himself had been a beneficiary of their power. According to Plato, he was initiated into the "rites of love" by a priestess called Diotima. She revealed to him many of the things about love that became central to philosophy. Plato also writes about how the mysteries showed individuals what happens to the soul after death and it is not unlikely that his understanding of philosophy developed as a partial critique of the older versions of these rites, in this way.

After Socrates's death, he may well have traveled to Egypt, where he was initiated into another set of mysteries: the antique Egyptian rites of Osiris. Only, the experience was not entirely satisfying. To his developing mind, the rites had become ossified and mechanical, seemingly mummified. The obsolescence prompted a desire to reignite their power for an increasingly introspective age and Platonic philosophy was, in part, the result.

The mysteries certainly became increasingly popular in the centuries that followed the death of Socrates. The most famous, at Eleusis, had to be taken into state control to manage the numbers. Thousands were taking part every year. It's reckoned that, in time, a majority of Athenian men would have been through this initiation, as well as some women, slaves and foreigners. Walter Burkert, the great scholar of ancient Greek religion, notes that at their peak, their promise of mystical rebirth would have been a major selling point, alongside the more general sense that the mysteries offered a chance to do something other than perform the obligatory rites of the city. They were an act that an individual could choose for themselves.

They consisted of ceremonies and trials that generally took place at night and amidst strict secrecy. It was an ordeal to undergo them, exposing the individual to disorientation and fear, but thereby precipitating profound shifts of perspective in those who took part. They presented a threshold and, in this way, had the same effect as the philosopher's *aporia*. Importantly, they were in principle open to all regardless of social position or status. It's another indicator that the lives of individuals were being recognized and valued. The main requirement was to understand the Greek language in which the rites were conducted.

Plutarch, the Roman writer of the first century CE, described the mysteries at Eleusis in the following way:

> Wandering astray in the beginning, tiresome walkings in circles, some frightening paths in darkness that lead nowhere; then immediately before the end all the terrible things, panic and shivering and sweat, and bewilderment. And then some wonderful light comes to meet you, pure regions and meadows are there to greet you, with sounds and dances and solemn, sacred words and holy views; and there the initiate, perfect by now, set free and loose from all bondage.

Cicero, for one, regarded the mysteries as the greatest of ancient Greece's many legacies. The initiation equipped the individual with the means to live happily and die with hope, he explained.

The Greek mind woke up. Where the hero of Homer had felt him- or herself to be manipulated by gods, the philosopher of Hellenism hoped to possess their own subjectivity. Where sculptors before Pheidias had produced figures that evoked an undifferentiated sense of presence, he and his successors carved figures that projected awareness. Where the poets of the old world spoke of fate and invasion, the playwrights of the Athenian awakening fostered the experience of conscience.

The philosophers nurtured new hopes of personal salvation, of insight into life and death, of direct knowledge of the transcendent. They developed practical trainings that fostered a sense of self which knew itself to be connected to the cosmos and the divine. This reciprocal participation introduced human beings to notions such as the soul, the value of education, and the wonder of contemplating earth and heaven.

* * *

It was this Hellenistic civilization that found its way into the center of the Jewish way of life following the conquests of Alexander. The people of Israel were, then, exposed to Greek ways in commerce and culture. Jews started to meet in a new place, the local synagogue, a "house of prayer" that revolutionized religious practice: the spread of synagogues made reading and learning as important as sacrifice and ritual. Greek translations of the formerly Hebrew Scriptures, such as the Septuagint, became the standard texts, the Septuagint being ascribed a miraculous status. The Greek language was adopted widely, too, so that later Jewish writers, like Paul and Philo, used it fluently and without question as the appropriate language in which to discuss the revelations of God. Philo taught that Moses "had reached the very summit of philosophy," and that Greek philosophy was the working out of the Mosaic teachings.

Hellenism wasn't accepted by all. Josephus could be critical of the Greeks, though in so doing he recycled the jibe of a Greek, Plato. The philosopher had said that his people were temperamentally young and preferred what is different and new to what is old and wise. Jews who had assimilated Greek mores and culture could be attacked by their zealous cousins, too.

But for all that a few tried to rend the two cultures asunder; Hellenism and Hebraism accommodated and informed one another. "The enigmatic passages in the Mishnah and later rabbinic texts about attempts to limit the teaching of Greek and Greek wisdom to Jewish children are exceptional in a history of general acceptance," writes historian, Martin Goodman.[31] "All that can validly be asked is whether some Jews imbibed the Greek culture more than others, and to what extent variations can be traced between places and over time."

It particularly affected the prophetic tradition, nowhere more so than with the appearance of the genre of the apocalyptic. Individuals like Amos and Hosea had declared God's judgment on the kings of Israel. In the Hellenistic period, though, prophecy widens its horizons. Instead of God's judgment being expected in the immanent future of the here and now, it transitions to being expected eschatologically, which is to say at a moment when history will come to an end.

It's a shift directly linked to the focus on the divine name and the prominence of interiority because what forms is an anticipation of a day of judgment when the individual will stand before the throne of God. It will also be a day of anxiety. It's as if the later, apocalyptic prophets begin to discern that a personal relationship with God may contain a promise of salvation. Apocalypticism became a spiritual milieu within which individuals wrestled with what such salvation might require. It took hold of people's minds as they reviewed their experience of God and their own righteousness. The florid visions that followed are a direct expression of an intensification of this sense of self and its, at times, intolerable fears. The emergence of eschatological hopes was powered by a raging call for fairness, which the righteous individual could now demand.

Take the book of Daniel. This second-century BCE text, probably the youngest in the library of canonical Jewish scriptures, offers a mature apocalyptic vision. It borrows and retells earlier stories, notably that of Daniel in the lions' den, the details of which clearly resonate with the period of exile. But it also begins trends such as reforming angelology. For example, Daniel transforms the local gods of original participation into national guardian angels, Michael becoming the special protector of Israel (Daniel 10:13).

It was partly in response to a period of monstrous oppression that the Jews were suffering at the time, particularly under the disastrous successor to Alexander, Antiochus IV Epiphanes. In a grim misappropriation of the notion that a person can transmit the divine, his name meant "god manifest." Aside from slaughtering Jews who refused to recognize his magnificence, he is the one who erected the "abomination of desolation" in the temple (Daniel 11:31). Daniel cries with outrage, fear of divine justice, and yearning for an end to the transgressions and desecrations. Only apocalyptic prophecy can fully express the shock, although simultaneously, what Daniel sees is often too much for him to bear. After one vision, he lay sick for days, though he also saw "the appearance of a man" who might help him understand, discern and tolerate the revelations (Daniel 8:15–16). That individual was a sign of hope to an individual who was deeply troubled by his exposure to injustice and to God.

The Hebrews were not alone in feeling such stresses. It was a mood felt across the Hellenistic world. An Egyptian, known as the Oracle of the Potter, predicted in the third century BCE that a righteous king would come to overthrow the evil of the age. At that time, the pious who had previously died would be raised again. Or there's the Zoroastrian Oracle of Hystaspes who, rather like Daniel, imagines a future conflagration in which the corrupt will be exterminated because God will hear the individual voices of the righteous.

The inner dimension of such visions had been earlier picked up by Plato. In his dialogue, the *Gorgias*, he describes why Zeus decided to stop mortals knowing about the time of their death. They were repenting and reforming themselves at the last minute, which meant that they could ensure being sent to the Isles of the Blessed, and avoid the hell of Tartarus to which the judges of the living might otherwise have condemned them. By withholding knowledge of their last day, Zeus could ensure that mortals would take responsibility for their actions throughout their lives. This is what is expected of a spiritual self.

An interesting group of radical Jews began developing parallel ideas. They were the Essenes, who were a footnote in history before being re-allotted a central place following the discovery of the Dead Sea Scrolls at Qumran in the second half of the twentieth century. There is much scholarly discussion of their significance. It seems that they were part of a rich array of sectarian groups who flourished in the Greek and, then, Roman periods, before they were wiped out by the Romans in the first century CE. They offer another glimpse of the interplay between

Hellenistic and Jewish hopes, and the trend of a strengthening sense of self.

For one thing, the Essenes seemed to have turned their backs on the temple, instead stressing personal virtues and practices like baptism. They developed a powerful sense of the dynamics of truth and injustice fighting "in the hearts of men," as one scroll puts it. This personalization of religious struggles has been likened to what we might now regard as forms of psychometric types.[32] The wicked heart was said to manifest itself in thick and hairy bodies. The good heart showed itself in slender and glowing characteristics. There were other categories of people in-between. Whatever you make of such physiognomy, it speaks of a self-alertness that counseled "constant introspection," as Philip Jenkins puts it.[33]

All in all, the meeting of Jews and Greeks was immensely energizing. Hopes for personal forms of resurrection or immortality deepened. Anticipations of divine vindication for righteous individuals became established. Experiments in novel forms of religious subjectivity spread. The Jews were experiencing an ingathering of participation focused on the distrust of idols that was simultaneously a centripetal heightening of their participation in God's life. "[God] had now only one name – I AM – and that was participated by every being who had eyes that saw and ears that heard and who spoke through his throat."[34] Barfield goes so far as to wonder whether Jews might have heard the name of God when they spoke their own name. He notes that the Hebrew word for "Jew," which by now had become an ethnicity not merely a nationality, may be rendered YHWDI. "The texture of the language hints that a devout Jew could hardly name his race without tending to utter the Tetragrammaton. Written, as all Hebrew words were, without vowels, when any true child of Israel perused the unspoken name, YHWH may have seemed to come whispering up, as it were, from the depths of his own being!"[35]

By the first century CE, Judaism had become thoroughly pluriform, often in dispute with itself. Personal crises over what it might mean actively to dedicate oneself to a righteous God became common and, after the destruction of the Second Temple in 70 CE, many Jews continued to move in radical directions along this trajectory. You could say that the interiorization of their religion saved them a second time. Now, as what is called Rabbinic Judaism, it developed a "normal mysticism." This was about discerning Yahweh's presence in the minutiae of life, in experiences highlighted by the demands of the law that reached into every part of the day. The rabbis taught that Yahweh spoke to each person as he or she was able to comprehend so that God became an almost purely subjective experience, with each person experiencing God's "I AM" in a way that matched their sense of self. The identification of the rabbis with God became so strong that when they again rehearsed the old stories of Yahweh's saving acts, they could say something that would have shocked their post-exilic forebears: "Thou, Lord, has redeemed thyself."[36]

Philosophical adepts, inspired by the Greek tradition, continued to cultivate themselves and offer their advice deep into the Roman period, as well. It was not until long after the Sack of Rome in 410 CE that Plato's Academy was closed for the last time, in 529 CE.

But by then another movement, who were also called philosophers for a while, had joined the task of developing human consciousness. They were also first-century CE Jews, though they turned in a different direction from their Rabbinic cousins. They secured the shifts of mind that had been emerging, took further steps that definitively shaped it, and found ways of spreading its benefits beyond the elites to the masses. They did so because they came to believe that a man had lived whose life itself marshaled and displayed these inner developments. They argued that this individual could and should be regarded as manifesting the clearest pattern for such hopes. Indeed, he brought it to fulfillment. He incarnated the inside of the cosmos so that God could be seen in his individuality. They were the followers of someone they believed had perfectly embodied and taught it all, the Hellenistic Jew, Jesus.

Chapter 5

The Secret Kingdom

Much of what Jesus stood for suited the stormy spiritual weather of the first century CE. Born into a world of religious foment, he was an astute observer of the waves of change. But there's more to him, much more, which is why he's remembered when other prophets and sages, contemporary with him, are forgotten.

He imbibed the wellsprings of the Greek and Hebrew past in Hellenistic Judaism, distilled their inner potential and manifested the extent of their meaning. It led his followers to perceive that here was someone not only expressing but living a life of all possible fullness, though they simultaneously wrestled with just what that might mean. The New Testament is frank about it. His disciples routinely misunderstood the consciousness he inhabited. They struggled to transition to it themselves and, I suspect, the gospel authors strove to capture that struggle in what they wrote so that reflecting on it might facilitate the conversion of their own readers. To this extent, they were like Plato when he chose to write dialogues. They wanted to convey a revelation not make a record.

That said, I discovered something that quite surprised me as I was researching this book: the quest for the historical Jesus, as the efforts to discern the details of his life are known, has led to many strikingly settled details which support the conviction that this Galilean rabbi lived a decisive life at a critical moment in the development of human self-perception. The scholarship can help to see how something definitively constellated with him and cast it in a vivid, fresh light. It reveals the heart of the meaning of Christianity.

* * *

Jesus was born into an artisan class of modest means. His family lived in the village of Nazareth, within easy walking distance of the bustling Greek city of Sepphoris, a growing metropolis that was probably an important source of employment. He would have been educated in the synagogue, the place of learning that had become widespread and popular in the couple of centuries before his birth. The gospels say that he was manually skilled, a carpenter, though that description also has a hidden meaning: it may refer to him being widely recognized from early on as a wise teacher (Mark 6:3).[37]

He was a crafter in truth, though his background was unpretentious, and that was, I suspect, valuable. It meant that he could be alert to the currents of the times without being overly burdened by social expectations. His marginal status lent him the inner freedom of those who are neither total outsiders nor the constrained elite. He had the right roots, as did others. Socrates had been an impoverished freeman whose family trade was stonemasonry. He could, therefore, benefit from the awakening of fifth-century BCE Athens and at the same time question what it meant. Or there's Paul, Jesus' great interpreter and another pioneering artisan, a tent-maker from the city of Tarsus. According to the historian Strabo, Tarsus was generally reckoned to rank third when set alongside the great cultural centers of Alexandria and Athens. It was an inferior but not insignificant city that, as a birthplace, served Paul well.

Jesus' relatively brief appearance as a public figure, which lasted between one and three years, followed his meeting with John the Baptist. The ancient historian Josephus calls John, "a good man." He was a charismatic individual, who could be found in the desert on the far side of the River Jordan. A powerful speaker, Josephus continues, he called people to righteous lives, the familiar theme amongst contemporary preachers. He was possibly influenced by the Essenes. Submitting to his baptism was the sign of responding positively to his call, and he was successful. He gathered followers, some of whom still exist, and the publicity he garnered is probably what led to his execution by Herod Antipas just before 30 CE. The authorities were always nervous of spirited individuals who could stir up crowds because religious gatherings are difficult to control. It was probably the same ability that, at one level, led to Jesus being arrested and killed.

John stirred Jesus up. But what Jesus discovered, or had confirmed, was a vocation that went well beyond John. As the historian, Robert Knapp, summarizes: "After his baptism, Jesus stayed in order to meditate and gain focus for his personal message. He emerged from the wilderness as a charismatic leader in his own right."[38] His consciousness of himself and God had been raised. It was his moment to speak to the pious revivals, righteous discontent and apocalyptic visions flaring all around. He was to address the demands of Yahweh's requirement to love God with the totality of one's being and recognize what a profound difference that can make to human experience.

He was of his times and exceeded them, and teasing out the difference is precisely what can illuminate the secret side of what he embodied. This is the way to take things further so, first, it's worth asking what he shared in common with the teachers of his age.

* * *

An obvious similarity is that he took up an itinerant, ascetic way of life. "Foxes have holes, and birds of the air have nests; but the Son of Man has nowhere to lay his head," he is reported to have said (Luke 9:58). Leading scholars like John P. Meier have discussed how other Jews like John had peripatetic callings, as did non-Jews like the roving Cynics, whom Jesus was almost certainly influenced by, another scholar, John Dominic Crossan, has argued. Cynics would have been known in Sepphoris as they stood back from everyday life, much as Socrates had done when he distanced himself from the requirements of Athenian citizenship. In so doing, they could see the deeper possibilities that the received wisdom obscured. A degree of inner detachment is good advice, particularly if you become disenchanted with the clamorous obsessions that dominate the headlines and sense that behind them lurks spiritual poverty, though the attitude was particularly significant two millennia ago because it marks another break from original participation. For David and Solomon, as for Homer, there had been no distinction between the spiritual and the temporal, the divine and the political. To honor the king was to honor God. But reciprocal participation promises a different kind of freedom and how you relate to the secular world is one domain where that's worked out.

Jesus was strong on this point, as is remembered in one of his best-known sayings. "Render to Caesar the things that are Caesar's, and to God the things that are God's" (Mark 12:17). This balance of being in the world but not of the world, to use John's version of the formula, was crucial (John 15:19; 17:14–16). Paul saw it as central too: "Do not be conformed to this world, but be transformed by the renewing of your minds, so that you may discern what is the will of God – what is good and acceptable and perfect" (Romans 12:2). To see more, you need space. Rendering to Caesar the things that are Caesar's, and to God what's of God, is not just practical advice. Spiritually, it's fundamental.

Jesus' stance towards the Jewish law picked up on the revisions of the Deuteronomists and pushed in the same inner direction. He taught the Torah in the intimate way that focuses the Shema on the relationship between the individual and God: "Hear, O Israel: The Lord our God, the Lord alone. You shall love the Lord your God with all your heart, and with all your soul, and with all your might" (Deut 6:4–5). As he stressed: "Love the Lord your God with all your heart and with all your soul and with all your mind and with all your strength ... Love your neighbor as yourself. There is no other commandment greater than these" (Mark 12:31). He saw it was a crucial invitation that is wise to take up (Mark 12:34), and so was in line with those who had realized that a new relationship with the divine sprang from personal insight and devotion. "[Jesus] intensified the Torah primarily by applying it to internal dimensions of the human psyche: to dispositions, emotions, thoughts, and desires," explains Marcus Borg.[39]

It's also in line with the so-called Golden Rule which, by Jesus' time, had become a staple of moral consciousness. Treating others as you'd like to be treated yourself had replaced an eye for an eye, a tooth for a tooth. He also seems to have taken the extra step of teaching people to love their enemies, not only their friends (Matthew 5:44). He was not alone in that, either. Socrates had done as much.

What have come down to us as the beatitudes, the summary of his teaching that Matthew and Luke present in the so-called Sermon on the Mount, reflect similar concerns. Others, like the Essenes, used the beatitude teaching form, as the Dead Sea Scrolls attest. "Blessed is the one who speaks truth with a pure heart and does not slander with his tongue. Blessed are those who hold fast to wisdom's precepts and do not hold to the ways of injustice. Blessed is the man who has attained wisdom and walks in the law of the Most High."

These blessings, from one of the manuscripts found at Qumran, do reveal a difference, though, when compared with the beatitudes attributed to Jesus. About half of Jesus' begin by referencing groups of people who are materially disadvantaged, those who are poor and hungry, as well as those who are conventionally pious, the pure in heart and the righteous. Like the Cynics, it suggests that Jesus detected a spiritual advantage in not having much. The Cynics taught and preached imperatives like not worrying about tomorrow and not bothering about what you wear or what you might eat and drink, and Jesus advised the same. It's another way of cultivating inner space or, to put it another way, it's where your heart is that matters. "It is easier for a camel to go through the eye of a needle than for someone who is rich to enter the kingdom of God" (Mark 10: 25). "You cannot serve God and wealth," he also said (Matthew 6:24). On the whole it's wise counsel to live with less, not more, if you hope to reorient your desires towards the divine. "Do not store up for yourselves treasures on earth, where moth and rust consume and where thieves break in and steal; but store up for yourselves treasure in heaven, where neither moth nor rust consumes and where thieves do not break in and steal. For where your treasure is, there your heart will be also" (Matt 6:19–20). Under reciprocal participation, attitudes and apprehensions are all. They measure the extent of divine awareness, the degree to which a person sees God.

More generally, it is who or what you are serving that is key, and being alert to the spirit of your devotion matters more than obeying the letter. In fact, obeying the letter can be a distraction from the personal conversion which is what really matters.

A more subtle side of this focus is that it meant Jesus' practical advice could vary in ways that, at a surface level, can seem contradictory. To the rich man, who had kept the letter of the Law but still felt incomplete, he said: "You lack one thing; go, sell what you own and give your money to the poor, and you will have treasure in heaven; then come, follow me" (Mark 10:20). But in the story of the Good Samaritan, which is about a character who also has means, a slightly different dynamic is highlighted.[40] The Good Samaritan was not enslaved by his wealth. He enjoyed the freedom of a liberated soul and, when it came to the money he had, he displayed indifference towards it. The important thing is to be free with it, and so free from its ties, and the parable is an example of detachment in action. The Good Samaritan could give and respond spontaneously, as

Jesus could, too. He associated with the wealthy as well as with the poor, in the form of "tax-collectors and sinners" (Mark 2:16), and welcomed being anointed with an ointment that cost more than an average worker might earn in a year (Mark 14: 5–6). Unlike the rich young man, he could live with riches coming and going. Socrates comes to mind on this front, again, because he manifested the same ease with poverty and wealth. He is remembered for wearing no shoes, on the one hand and on the other hand, for joining in with the regular ritual feast practiced in ancient Athens, the symposium. In fact, at these, he developed a reputation for being able to drink wine without becoming drunk on it.

I like the story of the twentieth-century Jewish holy man, Rabbi Yitzhak, which expresses the attitude. He would be showered with gifts and donations by his admirers, so much so that other rabbis became jealous. Asked how he attracted so much largesse, he replied that people sensed how he felt indifferent about money, and so they became indifferent to money themselves, leaving it with him. Such is the life of spiritual adepts.

It's an ability to engage with life at a different level from the material, and it lies behind Jesus' remarkable abilities as a miracle worker, as well, I sense. The gospels provide plenty of evidence for his ability in this area, recording over 200 incidents. It's unlikely so many would have got in unless he had been known for healing, exorcising and raising from the dead. Such powers arise from being loosed from the humdrum and aligned to the divine. You can then transmit an alternative consciousness. It may cause people not only to leave their money with you but also to experience psychosomatic shudders, sometimes bodily earthquakes that can alter things materially as an unexpected energy pushes out from within. Hence, healings happened.

They happen now and others, back then, found they gained the same abilities. Paul was to discover his presence produced such effects and some were said to be able to perform even that most impressive feat of raising the dead. There's Apollonius of Tyana, a philosopher who lived a few decades after Jesus. He is remembered as resuscitating a recently deceased girl in a way that echoes the story of Jesus' raising of Jairus's daughter (Mark 5:21ff). It is said that Apollonius touched her and muttered something that woke her up.

These individuals were in touch with another side of life's vitality and it could be felt whilst in their vicinity. The so-called miracles were natural by-products of it. The result was that Paul, Apollonius, Jesus and no doubt others could precipitate dramatically healing effects. These were people around whom extraordinary things occurred. But they didn't tell you much about what it was you'd witnessed or felt, just that a profoundly different perception of life was nearby – which, I suspect, explains why Jesus doesn't seem to have made much of the miracles himself. He knew they could easily become distractions, though they made people sit up and listen.

He was onto the shifts in the experience of being human that were active in the period. It is only to be expected that others sensed them, too. But what of his differences? How did he nudge things forward? This is where his radicality can begin to be detected, how he was pulling ahead of his times. It can be seen, first, in other more novel teachings.

* * *

A fundamental area concerns the widespread fervor and belief that divine forces would intervene to end history. The apocalyptic appealed because it meant that individuals who had followed God honestly and in spirit could hope to be vindicated and taken up to heaven. Conversely, the wicked would no longer be able to escape justice as they had in life.

Jews and Greeks alike had become fixated on such end days.

During the first century CE, the obsession was driven by the brutality of Roman occupation, much as apocalypticism had first arisen as a visceral response to autocratic Greek rule. It formed into a conviction that God must vindicate the wronged in a fiery righting of religious, social and political transgressions. The wheat would be separated from the chaff.

Jesus felt it. All the evidence suggests so. But his take on it departed from more common beliefs. A careful analysis of his remembered sayings has led to a robust proposition. It's not agreed by all scholars, but it's a mainstream view, and has the advantage of making profound spiritual sense. Jesus believed the apocalypse wasn't an event to anticipate at some moment in the future. Neither was it a wrapping up of things at the end of time. Rather, it was already happening. It was now underway. Which raises an obvious question: where is the dreadful act of divine justice taking place? Jesus' answer was startling. He believed that the apocalypse is an inner transformation. It's an arrival of the kingdom of God in the human heart.

In a distinctive way, he was further closing the gap between God and the individual, between the widest external reality and the deepest inner reality. The Deuteronomists had devised a program to try to do so. The Greeks had intuited it is possible by awakening to the shared nature of mind and *Logos*. Rabbinic Judaism developed a path, too. Jesus found another way of expressing and teaching it. His claim was that the righteousness that many thought would descend from the heavens would not, in fact, come down because that other country was already here.

It was hard to understand, let alone accept, but the assertion forced his followers to reconsider the longings that motivated their hope. He taught them that the anxiety that was embedded in the apocalyptic could be redirected so that, after a period of disorientation and uncertainty, they might discover an intensified participation in God. The right focus is not without but within. This is where human and divine realities meet. Jesus' shorthand for it was to refer to the kingdom of God or, less frequently, the kingdom of heaven. In the Synoptic Gospels of Mark, Matthew and Luke, he uses the phrase on more than 50 occasions.

It was a possibly unique part of his teaching, and Luke's gospel, for one, preserves his take on it. "The kingdom of God is not coming with things that can be observed; nor will they say, 'Look here it is!' or 'There it is!' For, in fact, the kingdom of God is within you" (Luke 17:21). Luke also has Jesus observe that, already, "the kingdom of God has come to you" (Luke 11:20).

In Luke and Matthew's gospels, it's implied when Jesus answers John the Baptist's query about whether he is the expected one. He quotes some of Isaiah's early hopes about people streaming to Mount Zion with the inference that it's finally happening now (Matt 11:2–11; Luke 7:18–23). Mark has a number of sayings that hint the new times have arrived (Mark 2:19–22), and Luke and Matthew record further sayings in which Jesus says "something greater than Solomon" is here, meaning God's wisdom is present; and "something greater than Jonah," adding in God's judgment – two further aspects that signaled the arrival of the kingdom (Luke 11:31–32; Matt 12:41–42). The Gospel of Thomas includes a similar take on the issue: "I have cast fire upon the world, and look, I'm guarding it until it blazes" (Thomas 10). It's not that the fire will be cast. It's already ignited.

What's doubly interesting is that these sayings run against what was clearly believed by the majority of Jesus' first followers. They strove to hold onto the traditional understanding. Presumably it was easier to grasp than the spiritualized view because it drew on the meaning of the end times that was routinely preached during the Hellenistic period. Hence, in his earliest surviving letter, the First to the Thessalonians, Paul anticipates being alive when he presumed Jesus would return. "For the Lord himself, with a cry of command, with the archangel's call and with the sound of God's trumpet, will descend from heaven and the dead in Christ will rise first. Then we who are alive, who are left, will be caught up in the clouds together with them to meet the Lord in the air" (1 Thess 4:16–17). In such moments, he pushes the arrival of the kingdom back into the future.

More confusingly still, there are plenty of warnings in the gospels themselves that clearly imagine an apocalypse to come. Mark, Matthew and Luke do something that Paul explicitly refused to do (2 Cor 12:4). They penned apocalyptic prophecies. Mark provides a case in point: "Then they will see the Son of Man coming in clouds with great power and glory. Then he will send out the angels, and gather his elect from the four winds, from the ends of the earth to the ends of heaven" (Mark 13:26–27).

The pull towards a cosmic catastrophe, as opposed to a reorientation of inner perception, was strong and remained so in the generations after Jesus' death. It takes time to reconfigure such expectations, which must be why the Revelation of John made it into the biblical canon, though only just. But all this indicates that Jesus had, in fact, reinterpreted the apocalypse and saw things differently. The kingdom of God is found within in a way that seals the individual's relationship with the divine. The sayings that express this insight could only have survived because, whilst not comprehended, they were known to have been uttered by him. When the gospels were written, in the latter half of the first century CE, they had become precious, if confusing, links back to Jesus and they weren't, therefore, to be tampered with. They were part of the secret, hidden – as it were – in plain sight.

There's historical as well as textual evidence that Jesus modified the meaning of the end times in this way. Close to apocalyptic hopes were rebel hopes. They were widely held amongst zealous Jews who wanted to overthrow the Romans, and they had good reason repeatedly to try to do so. Pontius Pilate, who governed Judea from 26–36 CE, the period spanning Jesus' public life and death, was a particularly harsh ruler.

Josephus reports that on one occasion he ordered protesting Jews to be clubbed to death by incognito soldiers who had hidden themselves in the crowds. But, for all his brutality, he was not without a discriminating eye.

For example, the Bible indicates that Pilate spotted the difference between Jesus and Barabbas, the rebel who all four gospels say was released in lieu of Jesus after his trial (Mark 15:6ff). With Barabbas, Pilate had instigated the standard retaliation for the leader of an insurrection: imprisoning him along with all his murderous co-conspirators. But when it came to Jesus, he was taken into custody alone. The disciples were left, free to flee. Pilate must have believed Jesus was a temporary threat to public order but not a challenge to the political status quo. The gospels also imply that Pilate wrestled with just what Jesus was about. This man didn't fit the categories the governor was used to, as he stood silently before him.

The story of Jesus overthrowing the tables of the moneychangers in the temple (Mark 11:15) must have been symbolic of this otherworldliness and could not have been dangerously riotous, else he would have been arrested and not released. Pilate realized therefore that, whatever he was, he was not an insurgent. Jesus' spiritual imagination was intense and unsettling but, when it came to secular concerns, fundamentally indifferent. The kingdom that concerned Jesus was not of this world, though it is also here (John 18:36).

* * *

I suspect that most of his first followers didn't get what he was driving at. The esoteric meaning of the kingdom went over their heads, though not completely. Paul, for example, could on occasion proclaim that clouds and judgment will descend, though he could also refer to Jesus as "the Christ" or anointed one, a kingly title and Greek equivalent of the Hebrew "messiah."

It implies that the king has already come, which means that he can't be on the way to coming. Then, in a further moment of insight, Paul could teach that the Christ was alive in him now (Galatians 2:20) and that the goal for Christians is to put on the mind of Christ (Philippians 2:5). Here, he came closest to Jesus, I believe. He found the secret way, the narrow road, the small gate.

It's a process of message distillation not dissimilar to that expressed in the story of Moses and the Golden Calf. The Deuteronomists recounted how the ancient Hebrews and Aaron could confuse the old gods with Yahweh, the one who had actually saved them from Egypt (Exodus 32:4). The story makes a point. Lacking the eyes to see, it was hard for them to tell the difference. This is what it's like when a new consciousness is emerging and it also illustrates the common religious mistake of solidifying subtleties and turning nuance into literal events. It's an attractive option. It relieves tension and sidesteps the difficult task of reconceiving, and so receiving, an alternative awareness of oneself and of God.

It's an error that goes on to this day, in my view. Fundamentalists, for example, remain keen on the rapture, presumably because the activity of wildly imagining a fiery future has a faux-purifying effect. It draws attention away from the misunderstandings and failings that might be found in the group, and exports them elsewhere, to the surrounding society, which is deemed evil. Each generation of brimstone preachers has a favorite target for the outrage. Whatever or whoever the current scapegoat might be, they are used to fuel the proclamation of a Parousia.

Liberal believers reify in a different way. Here, a secular version of the apocalyptic tends to dominate when the stress of responding to Jesus' inner message gets too much. For example, in the tradition I'm most familiar with, liberal Anglicanism, there's a pronounced tendency to convert the gospel into a running commentary on this-worldly politics and, say, the failure of advanced economies to deliver wealth justice. It implies that the kingdom is not yet here because relative poverty is on the rise or social mobility has grown stagnant. Liberal preachers offer the catharsis of moral outrage to their left-leaning congregants, and silence the rest in shame and guilt. Such sermons also, in the case of the established church, offer a convenient justification for its ongoing existence. "Civil society needs us," is the implicit message, which may well be right. Only, civil society doesn't seem to have been Jesus' concern and something crucial is lost when the gospel becomes focused on social, secular worries that become ends in themselves. Such a message excludes the possibility of any real transformation.

That lay at the heart of Jesus' innovation. He wasn't just reiterating what was on the way to becoming self-evident and obvious. He stood for something more: a thoroughgoing change in worldview and imagination. It's important to assert because when Christianity becomes a set of moral requirements, and the arrival of the kingdom is deemed remote, the way it offers drains of joy and power. The central promise of a discovered union with God, from which social action might well then subsequently flow, gets lost. My sense is that this loss is central to the declining appeal of Christianity today. It communicates that the gospel has nothing to offer that an ethicist couldn't say equally well and possibly much better. After all, the secular ethicist can do so without caveats that churches insist upon, such as excluding the love of gay men and women.

There are places in the Bible where Jesus' true meaning is to be found without reservation – notably, in John's gospel, the most developed early response to the essential point. It contains no apocalyptic material and, instead, frames Jesus' earthly life as itself a transcendent intervention, a kingdom that has already arrived. The *Logos* has come into the world though the world doesn't understand it (John 1:10). As to the future, this is liberated to open onto something more. John writes that the Spirit of truth will come to reveal things that cannot be understood now. It will bring an even more dramatic extension of insight (John 16: 12–13). The promise is of an experience of divine life that is a direct participation.

Jesus expresses this in John by repeatedly referring to his relationship with God as between a father and a son. He's deploying a common Semitic idiom: only a father and a son really know each other well.[41] It speaks of a reciprocity of knowing, Jesus implying that such mutuality, such a psychic bond, now bridges the gap between the divine and the individual. The son participates in the life of the father. And he didn't just mean for himself: "On that day you will realize that I am in my Father, and you are in me and I am in you" (John 14:20). It can happen now.

But then, as now, it was immensely difficult to gain this new perception. Early Christians struggled with it for decades. And that raises the question of how it might, against the odds, come about? How did Jesus try to foster it? The gospels have an answer because they remember another distinctive feature of Jesus' teachings: his parables. The New Testament records over forty. "He did not speak to them except in parables," the Gospel of Mark reports (Mark 4:34). "That no one else in the beginnings of Christianity has a similar or even a nearly similar reputation can only mean that this too was a characteristic feature of Jesus' mission," argues James D.G. Dunn.[42] And parables function in a particular way. They work to awaken.

* * *

Recall the hyperbolic and ironic form of the sayings and stories that Jesus composed and coined. There's the remark about the rich, the camel and the eye of a needle. There are many others. "Is a lamp brought in to be put under the bushel basket, or under the bed, and not on the lampstand?" (Mark 4: 21). "The kingdom of heaven is like a merchant in search of fine pearls; on finding one pearl of great value, he went and sold all that he had and bought it" (Matthew 13:45–46). "If a shepherd has a hundred sheep, and one of them goes astray, does he not leave the ninety-nine on the mountains and go in search of the one that went astray?" (Matthew 18:12). "No one can enter a strong man's house and plunder his property without first tying up the strong man; then indeed the house can be plundered" (Mark 3:27). Mark Twain's famous remark that there is only one joke in the Bible, and it is a poor one, has been a curse. It's obscured the fact that Jesus was a master wit. A camel can't go through the eye of a needle, period. No one would think to put a lamp under a bed to start with. Only a foolish merchant would bet everything on one pearl. Only a foolish shepherd would leave the ninety-nine to go astray. What's plundering a house got to do with finding God?

But when the interior nature of Jesus' message is born in mind, as an invitation to see the kingdom, his wit immediately makes sense. At one level, irony and humor are a way of resisting being taken literally, a literalism that perpetuates the status quo, maintains established views on matters such as the apocalyptic, and alters no one's awareness of things. At another level, it pressures his hearers to search within themselves. As he frequently remarked: "The reason I speak to them in parables is that 'seeing they do not perceive, and hearing they do not listen, nor do they understand.' ... But blessed are your eyes, for they see, and your ears, for they hear" (Matthew 13:13, 16). What he wanted to reveal could not be brought into plain sight because he was nurturing the sight that might see it. It could not be summarized in a neat doctrinal formula or upright moral creed or reassuring social program. It could only be understood following a change of view. When stirred up, then they might comprehend.

The parables conveyed the secret or mystery of the kingdom

(Mark 4: 11). Jesus' purpose was to bring about the capacity to grasp it, to catalyze and so accelerate what was unfolding. It's why he was said to have taught as one with authority, unlike his contemporaries who, presumably, didn't quite know of what they spoke (Mark 1:22). They merely reported. But Jesus sought to secure what the scribes and prophets since the exile had been reaching towards, alongside what the philosophers had been developing.

His aphorisms were designed to initiate it, the word "aphorism" coming from the Greek for "shaking horizons." A good one, such as likening the kingdom of God to a mustard seed (Luke 13:18) or to the yeast in some dough (Luke 13:20), lodges in the mind. Like an earworm, it won't let you go until you wrestle its meaning from it, when it gives you its blessing. That happens when mental horizons shift.

Barfield thought extensively about how parables work and noted that it's a paradoxical teaching method because, in order to understand a parable, you need almost to have already got its message. You need to be primed, to be ready for it. Take the parable of the sower, which Mark records as the first one (Mark 4:1–9). It tells of a sower scattering seed. Some of it falls on the path, and birds eat it. Some of it falls on rocky ground, where it sprouts quickly but then withers in the Sun. Some of it falls amongst thorns, where the seedlings are choked. Some of it falls on good soil, where it grows and flourishes. "The sower sows the word" Mark has Jesus go on to explain (Mark 4:14), which does and doesn't take root.

Familiarity can blind you to how difficult it would have been to fathom what it meant. "Do you not understand this parable? Then how will you understand all parables?" Jesus says, presumably troubling the already troubled disciples (Mark 4:13). I imagine they realized this much: that he wasn't offering a prose commentary on farming. But what they perhaps missed is that the parable is not designed to be understood but rather to convert. It is a poetic prompt that, like nicking a seed, might cause the word to sprout in their hearts. It's like an initiation that draws the meaning from the interior life of the imagery and, thereby, alerts you to the interior life within you. Jesus couldn't simply inform the disciples about the kingdom of God, any more than a person who lives in a black and white world could be told about the color red.

The transition is a "violent change," akin to a rite of passage.[43] Teachers will have a sense of that violence if they've ever made the mistake of using an idiom incomprehensible to young minds. "Class, I've a bone to pick with you!" "Alex, you've cut off your nose to spite your face!" "Today we are going to kill two birds with one stone!" Uttering such incantations to children too young to understand will confuse them and might make them cry. They just won't get it. Once the hearer does, though, things change. A felt understanding emerges. Barfield reckoned it's a process that takes place in roughly three steps.

The first is to leave old perceptions and assumptions behind. It's another manifestation of the withdrawal of participation, of stepping into the wilderness, smashing the idols, and the *aporia* of not knowing. There is no hope of understanding the parable for those who refuse to do that. They'll be stuck with apparently trite images of sowers and seeds. Explanations won't help either. They lead either to further misunderstandings, as happens when the parable of the sower is interpreted as a clunky allegorical injunction to evangelize, "to sow the word"; or to irritation, as Jesus himself found, in the characters the gospel writers refer to as the scribes and the Pharisees.

However, if it's possible to contemplate the possibility of not knowing, a second step might be made. The hearer becomes expectant, daring. Their imagination is fired. Moved to a threshold, they gain a sense of anticipation that something previously hidden is coming to light.

In other words, parables can connect with the zeitgeist and

simultaneously, subtly rewire it. In fact, Jesus probably couldn't have achieved this effect much before the first century CE. "[H]e needed something that would come part of the way to meet him; some soil prepared and thirsty for the seed he came to sow; some souls for whom his Gospel, though new and startling, would yet, owing to their predispositions, not be so new as to seem wholly meaningless," Barfield explains.[44] Jesus wouldn't have connected with others before about then, though he also needed to bring his message before the soil had become overwhelmed by the tempestuous enthusiasms of mystery religions and apocalyptic rage. "The time is fulfilled, and the kingdom of God has come near," Jesus said (Mark 1:15). All was ripe. And when the time is right, a third step becomes possible. From unknowing and expectancy, the hearer of a parable might come to see.

The experience is not so much of getting it as being got by it. There is a quality of grace in the transition. Following the phases of despair, puzzlement and bewilderment, comes an influx of perception. The kingdom that, in reality, was always present reveals itself to the opened mind and therein lies its power. The individual discovers they know. A parable is understood not because it is explained but because it suddenly seems a given. It reveals what is the case and that is now affirmed and incorporated.

* * *

On some occasions, Jesus' use of wit and parable come together with a particularly disorientating effect, and correspondingly heightened potential for change. One example is the parable of the unforgiving servant, as it is often unhelpfully called (Matt 18:23–34). In it, Jesus tells a story about a king who decides to settle accounts with his slaves and, finding that they owe him much, releases them from their debts, one by one. At first, it sounds as if Jesus is offering a predictable homily on how people should forgive each other, in imitation of the good king. That's not a bad thing to do and it seems, at first, to be how Matthew sets it up. Except, there is very good reason to doubt this is what Jesus originally meant. The details of the story are less tidy, more unruly. In particular, he describes how the king is owed quite outlandishly large amounts of money by one of his slaves. The amount is "ten thousand talents" (Matt 18:24).

A talent was the largest unit of money at the time. Ten thousand, or *myrias* from which we get "myriad," was the largest number in the ancient Greek language. It's as if Jesus had said a googolplexian. The amount he is referring to is barely conceivable. It's too large to count. And yet, in the story, this is the order of magnitude of the debt that the slave owes the king.

It's ridiculous. Jesus must have meant his hearers to be bamboozled by it, stripped of any bearings by which to assess the story's meaning. It's more than an average worker in the first century could have earned in hundreds of thousands of years. It's way more than the tax-take of a domain or province. The implication is that Jesus chose a number that precluded rationalizing the parable, which is to say that he meant it to make an impact, not to be a preachy illustration of a behavioral message that could be decoded in a few moments. When parables are so reduced, they end up changing nothing because they cease to be invitations to partake in a new experience and instead are felt to have a finger-wagging "palpable design" upon you, as T.S. Eliot memorably put it. They constrain not liberate.

That's the temptation, to interpret the king as God and the ludicrously indebted slave as merely a heavily indebted slave. Under that reading, the story goes on to tell about how the slave (you or I) bumps into another slave (a neighbor or colleague) and demands that whatever is owed to him be repaid (i.e. beware you're not like him in not forgiving your neighbors as well). The king (God) hears of it and brutally chastises the unforgiving slave (the punishment we deserve for not forgiving as we have been forgiven). It becomes a verbose tale. It reduces a jolting parable to a prose allegory. It deadens the impact.

If, though, you hold onto the mad sum of money the slave is said to owe, the parable raises the possibility that Jesus wasn't really interested in debts and money at all. Rather, he's taking a scenario familiar to all in a slave economy, exaggerating it, and utterly transcending it. It's as if he's implicitly referring to the infinite value of life, which is way beyond price. If you only had a glimpse of how much that is worth, he is pleading. You wouldn't be bothered about what your brother or sister owes you. Your life wouldn't be shaped by meanness, the need for security, monitoring what you're owed, competitiveness, control. Your inner sight might become fixed on something else entirely. And that could liberate you. If you perceived this in your heart, then you would be free to live and forgive everything. You'll become aligned with God.

Another parable that works similarly is the laborers in the vineyard (Matt 20:1–16). Jesus makes the central point, with dry humor, by telling of how the laborers in this particular vineyard are all paid the same wage at the end of the day, no matter how many hours they've worked – and some have worked for one hour only. Unsurprisingly, the longer working laborers complain. But, they shouldn't. As Jesus concludes: "The last will be first, and the first last."

There is, again, a moral reading of the tale, which laboriously explains that followers of Jesus should subjugate themselves and not complain when they aren't paid what they are due. They should put themselves last. But the shock reading is very different. It advocates anarchy. It pays scant attention to decency, let alone wealth justice. It's attitude – First? Last? Who cares! There is a different kind of order at play that can only be discerned at the hidden level. But it prompts freedom. "For my yoke is easy, and my burden is light," Jesus also said (Matt 11:30). Personally I think that's one of the most important things he ever said.

Consider one more case. The so-called parable of the talents uses exorbitant amounts of cash again (Matt 25:14–30). This time, a property-owning master is said to be setting off on a long journey. Whilst he's away, he entrusts three slaves with three sums of money. To the first, he gives five talents, to another two, and to the last, one. The first slave invests the money, so that when the master returns, he has ten fabulous talents to offer back. He's declared good and faithful. The second one acts likewise and returns four. He too is praised. But the last one falls into a panic. He buries the one talent and so only has one to give back. He's made nothing. The master condemns him fiercely and sends him to a place where there's weeping and gnashing of teeth. "For to all those who have, more will be given, and they will have an abundance; but from those who have nothing, even what they have will be taken away," Jesus avers.

In my experience, liberal Anglicans panic at this point. Read as a moral tale, it sounds like free market economics gone mad; as if Mrs Thatcher took Jesus as her guru. I've heard all sorts of interpretations that try to ease the discomfort. We're supposed to side with the last slave and feel sorry for him. We're supposed to interpolate a fourth slave who rejects financial investments. It's about taking risks or not passing the buck.

But perhaps it's not really about money at all but a wealth that materialism can't envision. If that kind of wealth is buried, pickled in reified traditions you might say, then it will be taken away. The vision will inevitably die. But if that wealth is invested, by staking your life on it, then its abundance will yield way more. Jesus indicated on many occasions that he was indifferent to money. He certainly wasn't interested in growth rates because, instead, he was immersed in a spiritual economy. In that kingdom, it's a truth that for those who have, what they have can only grow and develop.

Jesus must have realized the parables were likely to be

misheard. He'd have seen it happening before his eyes, an experience remembered in the frequent references to the disciples, and others, not understanding him. "Do you not yet understand?" (Mark 8:21). "Why does this generation ask for a sign?" (Mark 8:12). "Let anyone with ears to hear, listen!" (Mark 4:9). Some just didn't. The seed is consumed, withers and chokes, for all that, from this time on everyone has the potential to awaken. They live at the critical time, the opportune moment. The sower sows the seed indiscriminately. Its potential can be found all over the place.

Even an inspired gospel writer like Matthew can fudge the meaning. He had one eye on the kingdom, that much is demonstrably true, but another on the congregation for whom he was writing, and he appears often to have shaped and interpolated sayings as practical instructions for daily living. I suppose he had to. Possibilities here would include not taking each other to court to settle disputes (Matt 5:25), something I doubt Jesus would have commented on as an itinerant teacher living on the edge of civic life; and not using the traditional Jewish way of getting divorced (Matt 5:32), a ruling that contradicts Jesus' attitude towards the Law shown in remarks that are much more likely to be his own, such as: "The Sabbath was made for humankind, not humankind for the Sabbath" (Mark 2:27).

In other words, teaching alone, no matter how powerful and ingenious, is not enough. Alongside the reform of the apocalypse and the proclamation of parables, both of which point to a changing consciousness, practices are required, too. Jesus thought about them, as well.

Chapter 6

Christ Consciousness

Jesus' teaching was crucial, though it must have become clear that it was not enough. The participation in God he strove to communicate, and was directly to convey, needed more if it were to be instilled in the hearts of his followers. So, there was another important element in his public life. It wasn't so much about parables and preaching as about spiritual practice.

He recommended personal practices that were already in use but stressed their interior aspect, so as to nurture a steadier sense of the kingdom and facilitate the realignment with it. For example, he invited individuals to take up praying privately and individually, which must be why all of his recorded prayers, bar one, are expressed in the first person singular. This was relatively novel, even for synagogue-going Jews. "Whenever you pray, go into your room and shut the door and pray to your Father who is in secret" (Matthew 6:6). Similarly, he taught them to refocus in quiet places (Mark 6:31), as he himself had done in the wilderness (Mark 1:12–13), as well as to fast surreptitiously, "so that fasting may be seen not by others but by your Father who is in secret; and your Father who sees in secret will reward you" (Matt 6:17–18). He wanted to nurture an unmediated intimacy with God.

Calling God "Father" or "Abba" was adopting another contemporary Jewish habit and making it central because it captured the possibility of mutuality with the divine. He encouraged his followers to seek this experience, as his best-known prayer implies (it's the one expressed in the plural): "Our Father in heaven" (Matthew 6:9). He genuinely believed this is possible. "Ask and it will be given to you; search, and you will find; knock, and the door will be opened to you" (Matt 7:7).

And it was a strategy that worked. When Paul came to write his Letter to the Romans, in the mid-50s about 20 years after Jesus' death, the apostle agreed: "When we cry, 'Abba! Father!' it is that very Spirit bearing witness with our spirit that we are children of God, and if children, then heirs, heirs of God and joint heirs with Christ" (Romans 8:15–17).

There was another side to Jesus' spiritual exercises, ones that counteract the huge risks that a hope for divine awareness can bring. The prevailing sin, here, is pride and Jesus is remembered as having been very alert to it, particularly as it hides in people's intentions. He encouraged people to pay keen attention to them.

He clearly had a sharp eye for what goes on inside the mind. "Why do you see the speck in your neighbor's eye, but do not notice the log in your own eye?" (Luke 6:41) is a saying indicative of that. Today, that'd be called projecting, the subtle mechanism described by psychoanalysts that limits our lives because we become preoccupied with the lives of others. He knew that secret desires control life more powerfully than overt acts, a truth captured in the ferocity of other sayings on this issue: "If then the light in you is darkness, how great is the darkness" (Matt 6:23). That's true.

In the same way, he told his disciples that if the kingdom were within them, then they mustn't act as if their responses to the good news were furtive and would never be exposed. "For there is nothing hidden, except to be disclosed; nor is anything secret, except to come to light," he said (Mark 4:22). This indicates how to understand the gospel theme of judgment and is similar to the imperative that lies behind some of his most extreme and, apparently, moral decrees. He observed that the lecherous are adulterers (Matt 5:28). He proposed cutting off your right hand if it might be a cause of sin (Matt 5:20). He insisted: "Be perfect, therefore, as your heavenly Father is perfect" (Matt 5:48). Only, these are not literal statements. They're not supposed to be enacted as laws. They're another set of droll remarks with the serious goal of sparking the imagination. Heard in this way, they provoke a higher knowledge of what's good. They might nurture the best in us. "Where virtue is concerned we often apprehend more than we clearly understand and *grow by looking* [sic]," as Iris Murdoch put it in her discussion of Jesus' method of teaching.[45]

* * *

To put it another way, this is a focus on virtues, not morality, if morality is thought of as what is right or wrong to do, whereas virtues are thought of as developing the right habits of mind or characteristics of personality. They lead us to what's good by enabling us to participate in what's good, found both within and outside of us. They disclose reality and require imagination to practice. As Plato had argued, it's virtues that connect us to the divine. Morality merely imitates it.

Take a quality like humility. The moral version of humility will teach that it's about putting yourself last, or adopting an unassuming stance, or effacing yourself in favor of another. But seeing humility as a virtue casts it in a very different light. It becomes a type of receptivity. It is putting yourself in the lowest place in order that, like the sea, all of reality can flow into you. It becomes a habit of embracing, of opening, of participating. It's not about how you act in the world as much as how you welcome the world. The humble person can know all things because they can receive all things, whether good or ill. This is another part of the inner meaning of Jesus' remark that the first will be last, and the last first, because the "last," in this sense, experience life from the divine perceptive, as the inside of the whole world.

Virtues enhance freedom by enabling the individual to live skillfully. They unveil a type of knowledge that is discovered because of the quality of the life being led. They find the buried treasure. The person who has the virtue traditionally called temperance, meaning self-restraint, can engage with what happens calmly. The person with the cardinal virtue of prudence, or practicality, can respond wisely, moment by moment. Courage facilitates bravery, and justice is about engaging with others in mind.

Aristotle thought of virtues as a type of expertise. To be virtuous is to be like an archer who can always hit the target, whether they are on horseback or on foot, whether the day is windy or still. The analogy highlights another feature of virtues. They are learnt by making mistakes, as much as getting it right. There never was an archer who hit the target without previously, repeatedly failing to do so.

The traditional Christian virtues of faith, hope and love look similarly different when re-imagined in this way. Faith is about responding to life from a place of trust, as opposed to a place of certainty or control. Hope is about engaging with things without losing sight of what's good and best, even when things are dying and tragic. Love is about the "extremely difficult realization that something other than oneself is real," as Murdoch put it.[46] It is the ability to see the world and others by imagining the being of the world and others, not fantasizing that they are as we are. It's why showing someone love is really about giving them the space to speak and striving to understand.

Other virtues could be listed. The great virtue of the Stoics and Epicureans, equanimity, is a kind of steadiness. Or there are the virtues celebrated in eastern wisdom traditions. *Metta* is engaging with life so as to befriend it. *Ren* is about acting humanely; *li* gracefully. Plato thought of virtues as caught, not taught. The virtuous person encourages others to be so because he or she comes across as appealing and beautiful, uncalculating and undefended. Others want to know what they know. I imagine this was the kind of impact that Jesus had upon those around him.

Paul captures the sense when, in one of his most open

moments, he advised: "Whatever is true, whatever is honorable, whatever is just, whatever is pure, whatever is pleasing, whatever is commendable, if there is any excellence and if there is anything worthy of praise, think about these things. Keep on doing the things that you have learned and received and heard and seen in me, and the God of peace will be with you" (Phil 4:8–9).

* * *

We become what we see. It is a transvaluation of all values, a disruption of mindset and conventions. "There is nothing outside a person that by going in can defile, but the things that come out are what defile," Jesus said (Mark 7:15). This remark would have scandalized many hearers if they were inclined to understand piety as right religious action, the benefits of which moved from the outside in. Jesus stood for something seemingly irresponsible, the Spirit that converted, that was discovered to be resident in souls that worked from the inside out. This is what now mattered. It was what the times required.

When it works a *metanoia* takes place, to turn to another key word. It's usually translated as "repentance," but its real meaning points to a revolution of awareness. *Meta* means "beyond." *Nous* means "mind." When Paul talked of being transformed by the renewal of your mind (Rom 12:2), he was offering a more accurate rendition.

The psychologist, William James, catches the richer sense in the chapters from *The Varieties of Religious Experience* in which he discusses such moments of conversion. He describes minds having "hot" and "cold" zones. Hot zones are sources of inner dynamism. When accessed, they invigorate life. Cold zones breed indifference, blindness and passivity. So a mind is changed when a cold zone ignites. The person is converted if they allow their mind to re-orientate, to be drawn to the heat and light. "The best repentance is to up and act for righteousness, and forget that you ever had relations with sin," James remarks.[47] That's to admit the influx of grace; to realize that God is a gratuitous giver and that salvation is not attained but perceived and received. It's what the prodigal son realized and it's why the secret way is one of freedom.

The dynamic is also conveyed in the way the gospel writers tell the story of Jesus calling the disciples. He says "follow," and they do so. "As Jesus passed along the Sea of Galilee, he saw Simon and his brother Andrew casting a net into the lake – for they were fishermen. And Jesus said to them, 'Follow me and I will make you fish for people.' And immediately they left their nets and followed him" (Mark 1:16–17). I'm sure a neighbor, sitting on the banks of the Sea of Galilee, wouldn't have recounted it like that. Presumably, Simon and Andrew had been mulling things over for some time. They were men of their times, aware of impressive healers, pretender messiahs, roaming philosophers. But the terse account conveys the essential, psychological truth. With Jesus, they didn't so much reach a decision as something clicked.

* * *

His consciousness could be their consciousness. What had been shown in his life could be active in theirs. If the kingdom were within them, then it followed that the Spirit of God was within them too, a dizzying implication. "The first Christians clearly relished the thought that they could so pray to God and saw it as attesting their having been given to share in Jesus' own relationship with God," writes Dunn.[48] They were on their way to making Augustine's discovery, when he realized God as "more in me than I am in me,"[49] and that God was "waiting within me while I went outside me."[50] Or there's Meister Eckhart's even more direct claim: "My eye and God's eye is one eye, and one sight, and one knowledge, and one love."[51]

Jesus' disciples clearly came to regard him as not only teaching about God, as other prophets did; and not just channeling divine power, as other miracle workers could; but as illuminating a relationship with God. That is what distinguished him, at least in the eyes of some. They went so far as, somehow, to recognize him as being full of God. He was a divine human, as others had said of Moses, or alternatively he was greater, perhaps even greater than the highest angels whose being was so godly that they could be called "Lord."

Some scholars have concluded that people probably called Jesus "Lord" during his lifetime because, in conjunction with his powers and teaching, they felt his transcendent credentials were unmediated.[52] They must have glimpsed his transparency to divinity, and he must have felt it welling up from within him too, manifesting through him, reaching beyond him. The title then continued to be used following his death and resurrection, not least when Paul audaciously modified the Shema to include Jesus: "For us there is one God – the Father, from whom are all things and we to him; and one Lord, Jesus Christ, through whom are all things and we through him" (1 Cor 8:6). Paul also cites "hymns" to Jesus, such as the one in Philippians that says Christ Jesus "was in the form of God" (Phil 2:6). Philippians is reckoned to have been written in about 50 CE. The hymn must have already been known, and therefore in circulation, and so could plausibly have been composed around 40 CE or before, just a handful of years after Jesus' death.

That his proximity to divinity was detected is also suggested by the reaction of his enemies. The eye of his soul was clearly focused on a kingdom that was not of this world and that, in a way, made his opponents all the more mad. They couldn't touch it. They couldn't get to him. The Jewish leaders who rent their clothes at the seeming hubris, as the tension between them and him reached its climax, were right. It was blasphemy. Jesus was claiming that the sacred ways ordained in scripture were now being superseded. They no longer fundamentally revolved around the temple or the Law but the individual. But the scriptures had been pointing to this moment. After the centuries of preparation, the kingdom of God was at hand.

There's a more subtle reflection of this divine precipitation in the attitudes Jesus had about himself. For example, it's interesting that the Synoptic Gospels don't make direct claims about the divinity of Jesus, I suspect because they reflect how Jesus presented himself. He wasn't much bothered by what people made of him, and actively discouraged speculation. He tells the agitated spirits he casts out to keep quiet (Mark 1:25); the people he's healed to go back to their lives rather than be carried away by the miracle (Mark 5:19); and the disciples to be wary of how they talk about him (Mark 8:30). The most spectacular expression of his inner nature came in the moment of transfiguration and, to witness this showing, he took only three of them, Peter, James and John (Mark 9:2).

Scholars call it the "messianic secret." Several have argued Jesus tried to insist on silence as a political expediency, to avoid drawing the attention of the authorities. There may be something in that, though there's spiritual wisdom in it. To understand the meaning of Jesus' divinity is only possible after a "mental fight," to use Blake's phrase, an awakening of a receptive mind that is, in turn, a realization about yourself. It's like Moses's grappling with the nameless name. To understand what is meant by God's revelation, "I AM," he had to grow into his own I-consciousness.

It's the Deuteronomist's recognition that the presence of God is not known on the page of even the most sacred scripture, but is rather in the mind of the individual who is wrestling with the words on the page. The Synoptic Gospels were, therefore, written to imitate the effect of meeting the historical Jesus so as to form, not merely inform, their readers. They are texts designed to enable people to awaken not only to him but to themselves. They do not portray him issuing self-declarations, as if he went around asking people whether they accepted him as their personal Lord and Savior, but rather are focused on readying the soul for the grace of insight. This is why Jesus has the attitude about himself that he does in the Synoptic Gospels.

The gospel writer, John, took a different approach, though with the same intent. My feeling is that because of his community's more formed appreciation of the kingdom of God happening now and not at some future arrival point, he could state and develop what his fellows already knew. He could be explicit about Jesus' divinity, identifying him with the cosmic *Logos* in his opening verses, and going further by including two sets of seven sayings that converge on the name apart. "Truly, truly, I say to you, before Abraham was, I AM" (John 8:58). He was re-envisioning the older theophany of Moses in the most blatant manner. If Jesus were known within, if Christ consciousness were already your own, such statements could be made completely and received directly.

John complements the full disclosure of Jesus' divinity with heartfelt accounts of Jesus' human experience in another spiritually fascinating way. For example, he repeatedly portrays Jesus' distress. Jesus weeps when he gets news of the death of Lazarus (John 11:33). He is deeply disturbed that someone will betray him (John 13:21). He is violently troubled by his approaching death (John 12:27). This might be thought of as an odd reaction in an individual who knew of his identity with God. But it, actually, reflects the inmost truth of this awareness. It is only because Jesus was fully human, and therefore vulnerable to the harshness of mortal life, that he could know of his human kinship with God. Mortal life in all its aspects is the prerequisite for appreciating God's life. Suffering is part of the way. It doesn't get in the way.

This is an extraordinary claim. It's a fundamental revelation of Jesus' life and explains why he became so pivotal in the evolution of consciousness. Without the mirror of his complete humanity, divinity would not have been reflected in him. The creedal formula for Jesus' incarnation, that he was "fully God, fully man," took some centuries to articulate, but it was not an afterthought. It reaches back to the core of Jesus' inner life and articulates the truth of how it might now be possible to know God.

It may be why Jesus clearly preferred to refer to himself as "Son of Man," an idiom that can be translated to mean "a person like me," as opposed to "Son of God," a phrase that focuses on the divine aspect of the human soul, made in the image of God.[53] It emphasizes that it was because Jesus was individuated as a man that he was uninterruptedly transparent to God. He showed that our humanity is our path to the divine. We're now close to the core of the secret of Christianity and the meaning of the kingdom and it has revolutionary consequences.

* * *

Take death. As I've argued, our distant ancestors, dwelling in original participation, appear not to have felt that the difference between life and death was absolute. The dead lived with their ancestors and living people believed they would join them when they died. However, they had this sense because they did not feel themselves to be isolated individuals. Their life was always already intimately tied up with the life of others. Death was a transition, therefore, rather than an end, because at death someone was felt to be returning to the life of their kin or tribe with which they had, all along, been sharing.

There is the possibility of some movement between the two realms. Saul thought so when he ordered the Witch of Endor to summon the prophet, Samuel (1 Samuel 28:3ff). The first book of Samuel also declares that, "The Lord kills and brings to life; he brings down to Sheol and raises up" (1 Samuel 2:6). But this is not resurrection. It's a temporary, typically unwanted, bringing back – a haunting. Comfort was found by dissipating as a person and rejoining the collective of the ancestors.

This had begun to change with the emergence of a more individualized consciousness. As a sense of gathered, personal awareness formed, so could a perception of psychic boundaries. There a difference between what's me and not me, what's mortal and immortal, what's inner and outer. That becomes clearer. However, there's a price for such individuality. At death, it could seem that life would be lost because the innate sense of connection with the flow of life had been broken, or at least eclipsed. A growing fear of death accompanies the move from original to reciprocal participation. It's another facet of withdrawal.

It's why preparations for postmortem existence shifted. Socrates argued that the connection between life and death, without a loss of the gains of individuality, could be found once more if the individual could readjust their sight to appreciate eternal life in this life. In the *Phaedo* dialogue, for example, Plato portrays Socrates as ready for death because he has one eye settled on the side of life that doesn't die, which he has befriended in the here and now. "Those who philosophize rightly make dying their care," Socrates remarks. It's another aspect of philosophy as a way of life. The philosopher steps back from the commonplace fears of frightened mortals and awakens to a forgotten ground. They're facing death to discover life.

The later Hebrew prophets felt that they would stand before God and be awarded with a renewed life. For example, the resurrection of the dead starts to be clearly envisaged in prophets like Daniel. He has a vision of the dead who sleep in the dust of the earth waking, with some being restored and going on to everlasting life (Daniel 12:2). Alternatively, Ezekiel's vision of the valley of dry bones being enfleshed and vivified is reinterpreted during this period (Ezekiel 37: 1–14). It had originally referred to the restoration of the fortunes of Judah and Israel because

Ezekiel received it during the period of exile. But a few centuries on, it is re-imagined as referring to a truly novel possibility, one of personal resurrection for the righteous on the last day.

Within both approaches is the realization that readying oneself for the life beyond this life requires a practice constantly of letting go of the sense that you possess your own life. It's not yours to have but it is yours to cultivate.

Plato summed it up with the expression that to philosophize is to learn how to die. He saw that death had come to be greatly feared by his fellows because of the tendency to cling to life as if an inalienable right. But that fear was also a clue. Instead of fighting death, the philosopher might use the ups and downs of every day to become conversant with the edges of life. The relationship between sunrises and sunsets, what's understood and what's not understood, what works and what fails, what's temporal and eternal, can be consciously investigated. It is in the midst of life that we realize we participate in far more than just our own life. So, by understanding your humanity, you might understand how you share in what's good, beautiful and true, insofar as they manifest in your humanity. The philosopher awakens as they gain a capacity to attune to life, which brings in its wake a gradual attunement to the divine. As Plato explained in the *Timaeus,* it is through contact with mortal life that the soul recalls its immortal life because it learns that what's created and mortal is shaped by what's eternal and immortal.

But there's a paradox. This very conformation feels like dying because, in a sense, it is. It is dying to the narrow view that, unchecked, the individual spontaneously and tenaciously adheres to. We are inclined to imprison ourselves in a carapace of mortal fears and possessive desires.

In the Jewish tradition, this was talked about, too. As it was realized that God could be found in the holy literature of the canonical texts, the prophets had stressed that God asks for a different kind of sacrifice than those performed in the temple.

It's inward. "The sacrifices of God are a broken spirit. A broken and a contrite heart, O God, You will not despise" (Psalm 51:17). This holy offering up contains a parallel dynamic to the philosopher's letting go. Such self-surrender made sense in the light of a person's "I am" reflecting the God who is "I AM." They themselves, as individuals, had all they needed to offer to God. What more could there be?

Jesus also intuited that the primary way of offering the righteous sacrifice is within the freely offered life of the individual. He expressed it, first, in parables. "Unless a grain of wheat falls to the earth and dies, it remains alone; but if it dies, it bears much fruit" (John 12:24). He also taught it aphoristically. "Whoever finds his life will lose it, and whoever loses his life for my sake will find it" (Matt 10:38). And then he enacted it, when he set his face to Jerusalem to die (Luke 9:51). "Those who try to make their life secure will lose it, but those who lose their life will keep it," he is recalled repeatedly teaching (Luke 17:33). Part of his uniqueness was to be the first consciously to render this truth crystal clear in his own death. Socrates had known he had to die because his daemon had told him not to escape the prison. Jesus knew he had to die because he understood what it was to embrace death. Barfield called it a "mystical fact."

But it was still death. Jesus, the individual who was with and was of God, knew what it was to be alone, cut off, apart from God. "My God, my God, why have you forsaken me?" he cries from the cross. (Mark 15:34). Without such desolation there is no knowing the depths of God because there is no knowing the depths of human experience. The philosopher, A.N. Whitehead, noted that such "scenes of solitariness" haunt the religious imagination. It's the central moment in any spiritual journey of weight and has subsequently been given many names from the dark night of the soul to having a breakdown. "It belongs to the depth of the religious spirit to have felt forsaken, even by God," Whitehead said.[54] But it is the forsakenness that opens up the depths.

In time, Platonists like Iamblichus were to agree. He affirmed explicitly that immortality is not gained by trying to escape mortal life but by conforming fully to mortal life, which in death can be recognized as replete with the timeless. The psychotherapist, Marion Milner, discovered a similar meaning to the crucifixion. She called it the "dramatization of an inner process of immense importance to humanity, a process which was not an escape from reality, but the only condition under which the inner reality could be perceived."[55]

Ever since the life and death of Jesus, the realization has been reiterated by multiple voices. By embracing human life, to the point of dying, we came to what is deathless in life. The cross on which Jesus died became such a powerful symbol, that might be dwelt on daily (Luke 9:23–25), because its shape signifies the joining of what is incomplete and disintegrated in human life with what's full and united in divine life. Meister Eckhart captures it joltingly: "The kingdom of heaven is only for the perfectly dead."

Many of the human stories that the gospels contain convey, upon reflection, death's secret. There is, of course, the passion of Jesus' death itself, so fully dwelt on by Mark, Matthew, Luke and John. And the gospels are chequered with smaller moments in which a symbolic death exposes new life, and anxieties and terrors are transcended. There's Mary's perplexed "yes" to the angel whose message overturns her life (Luke 1:38, 41). There's Peter's triple denial of Jesus and his bitter collapse, which becomes the ground zero of his awakening when he finally breaks free of his fear (Mark 14:66–72). Many of the healing miracles have the pattern embedded in them: a person at the end of their tether approaches Jesus, and he recognizes their broken spirit as the turning-point that establishes a different life. It's why the miracles can be read not only as natural healings but as spiritual transformations.

And there's one of the most initially perplexing moments from the morning of the resurrection. Mary Magdalene is in the garden and sees Jesus raised before he promptly says to her, "Do not hold onto me!" (John 20:17). It must have been almost impossibly hard to hear. Imagine her shock: "Noli me tangere!" And yet, this apparent rejection was her turning point. She realized he was her teacher – "Rabboni!" she replies – and, like all good teachers, he was not insisting she remain indefinitely dependent upon him but that she be free to live in the awareness of her own union with God. "I am ascending to my Father and your Father, to my God and your God," Jesus continues (John 20:18).

There are examples in the gospels of those who floundered or failed to see this Christ consciousness in themselves. You might say that Pilate was blinded by the worldview of which he was the head. His consciousness was fatally tied up with a kingdom that was of this world. The high priest's authority rested on a system of rituals and traditions and that blinded him, too. There's a profound irony in his remark that it is better for one man to die than that a whole nation should perish (John 11:48) because, in making it, he entirely misses how life can only really be known when the individual mystically dies. And then, there's Judas. Perhaps he tried to pull Jesus back from what appeared to him to be a looming dead end, only he then saw his master embrace it. Momentarily, he glimpsed the key to it all that he'd missed, and his error proved too much to bear.

Judas has been blamed. But who else, in the garden, saw it? I like to think that the famously abrupt ending to Mark's gospel is supposed to propel us to that moment and ask us what we see. The last incident recorded is the visit by the women to Jesus' tomb (Mark 16:1–8). They are met by a young man, dressed in white, who tells them not to be alarmed. But they are. They flee, terrified and amazed, which Mark accentuates with a final, hanging sentence: "And they said nothing to anyone, for they were afraid." It's as if this is the point at which they let go of all they thought they knew, were bewildered and undone, were lost and fully human. But they were also expectant. They were on the cusp of divine life, which Mark lets his readers feel in the silence with which he finishes. It's the space within which we might locate divine life in ourselves.

Barfield put it like this.

> Christ ... taught in a new and simpler way, and had then himself demonstrated, a truth which nearly every one of the Greek philosophers, including Aristotle, had been trying to say all their lives – that, in order to achieve immortality, it is necessary to "die" to this world of the senses and the appetites, and that he who thus "dies" is already living in eternity during his bodily life and will continue to do so after his bodily death. "Whosoever shall lose his life shall find it."[56]

It's therefore a mistake that much subsequent church teaching on Jesus' death has focused on treating it as a sacrifice that atones for sins. This is the logic of original participation. It's the ancient understanding of sacrifice, as an external action that produces prescribed results. It depicts Christianity as something to be gained from without rather than something perceived within, and also feeds a culture of dependency that, I think, is another of the most quietly unattractive aspects of modern Christianity for adult people. Better is another view that also runs through the tradition, sometimes called the sign or exemplary theory. On this understanding, sacrifice is not about anxiously securing benefits but is rather about cultivating a sacrificial attitude: the routine letting go and offering up of life. This inner habit re-orientates the sacrificer to the kingdom, and lets them drop into the life of God. It becomes a way of cultivating the detachment that enables the individual to be in the world but not entangled by the fears and distractions of the world – or, to put it in more modern terms, it's the detachment which recognizes that the ego makes a good and faithful servant and a terrible, tyrannical master, to recall a remark made by Carl Jung.

The moment by moment sacrificial act of will that puts to one side the will that would cling creates an inner space, a "naked nothingness," in Meister Eckhart's words. This is the "highest place," he continues, as it is a ready receptacle for God. Material things are regarded as valuable but not invaluable; emotions are richly felt but not so as to damage and overwhelm; worries about identity go, as the possessive tendency to assume I am this or that loosens. The risk of encasement in an isolated self erodes, reconnecting the person with the fountain of life, consciously to participate in what was its source all along. We shift from self-concern to the freedom of God. "He who binds to himself a joy does the wingéd life destroy. He who kisses the joy as it flies lives in eternity's sunrise," was Blake's brilliant summary. In this reading, sacrifice ceases to be an action and becomes a process of revelation and realization. It exposes the ground of life. It uncovers the incarnation of the divine within the soul. As the *Logos* incarnate, it comes to know that Jesus was the inside of the whole world, and that inside is there for us to know, too.

There is a central Christian act that acknowledges, nurtures and perpetuates these tender realignments: the re-enactment of the last supper. "For all who partake of the Eucharist first acknowledge that the man who was born in Bethlehem was 'of one substance with the Father', and that 'all things were made' by him; and then they take that substance into themselves, together with its representations named bread and wine."[57] The sacrament makes explicit what is implicit. Union with God can be found.

* * *

It is by revealing this existential bottom line that Jesus is the way, the truth and the life, and that no one comes to the Father "if not through me" (John 14:6). It's an inclusive not exclusive observation. "What has come into being in him was life, and the life was the light of all people," John also insisted (John 1:4). He makes clear what others up to this point had been formulating, and had partly succeeded in living. The difference is that Jesus' teaching and life fully combined to show what human flourishing looks like in what is now widely called the "Common Era." Like the Sun's light, God's life falls indiscriminately, over all. How could it be otherwise? The only question is whether that truth, in undoubtedly diverse forms, is recognized and appreciated.

Similarly, I think the so-called "great commission" with which Matthew ends his gospel (Matt 28:19–20) is inclusive, too. It's not an injunction to convert everyone to one particular creedal formulation of the truth. So far as I can tell, when Jesus reportedly said, "Go therefore and make disciples of all nations," Matthew was originally underlining that all ethnicities, not just Jews, could become conscious knowers of what Jesus made known. The gospel is not restricted. He didn't mean that all people must become signed-up members, and Christians mustn't rest until that target has been reached. That reading, and the title "great commission," seems to have become popular during the period of the British empire, when the Anglican church took on the imperial, and imperious, task of civilizing the world. The real truth is that, much as Jesus downplayed what people made of him in life and concerned himself with transforming their vision to perceive the kingdom in themselves, so too in his death he offers a demonstration that is an invitation. He shows that the main requirement is to be fully human as he was; a state of being that is indifferent to labels, formulations and tribes, Christian or any other.

* * *

If the most important truth of Jesus' life is that he was fully human, the seal of that truth is his resurrection. If he had historically lived, wisely taught and then nobly died that would have made him remarkable. That he lived, taught, died and then rose implies something further: he was what he taught without remainder.

That said, I don't think the resurrection is supposed to be treated as empirical evidence of his divine humanity. It's not as if someone with a smartphone, hurled back across the centuries, could catch the stone rolling away and post the verification online. The story of the empty tomb, which first appears in the Gospel of Mark, was told to illustrate the inner truth, not force acceptance of it. How could any story force anything anyway? Jesus' entire message had been about developing the eyes to see. This is what it is to be reborn.

I think it's for this reason that the empty tomb is not in Paul, who has the earliest surviving record of the resurrection, though Paul and the gospel writers are on precisely the same page (1 Cor 15:4–8). You might say Paul did not need to refer to it because Jesus appeared to him only after his death in an astonishing revelation (Gal 1:12). He saw Jesus that way directly, and had not known the physical body that was sown and died. But he knew what is raised and how that's different (1 Cor 15:44). It's a spiritual body, fuller and more real, like that of the angels.

Other accounts of the resurrection present things similarly. It's all about spiritual perception. That's the secret. Matthew describes the eleven disciples meeting on a mountain in Galilee after Jesus' death (Matthew 28:16–17). Jesus appears, resurrected, and some worship him. "But some doubted," the verse adds.

Alternatively, Luke has the story of Jesus appearing to two of the disciples on the road between Jerusalem and Emmaus. Jesus walks some of the miles with them, but without them recognizing him, even when he laboriously explains what had happened. Seeing him comes only with their communion (Luke

24:31), and even that assurance comes and goes. Later, Luke describes another appearance that terrifies the disciples. They think they are seeing a ghost (Luke 24:36). It's the depth to which you see that counts.

The clearest insistence that the resurrected Jesus is only fully seen by the eyes of the awakened soul comes in John's gospel, as we might expect. He tells the story of Thomas refusing to believe in the resurrection unless he touches the empirical evidence of a man with nail marks in his hands and a hole in his side. When Jesus appears a week later, Thomas gets his evidence, though Jesus comments: "Blessed are those who have not seen and yet have come to believe" (John 20:29). The implication is that evidence might actually distract you from inward sight. Nail marks don't prove anything. Seeing someone walking and talking after their death doesn't either, as the gospel writers must have realized when they included three other resurrections in their stories, those of Lazarus (John 11:44), Jairus's daughter (Luke 8:54) and the man from Nain (Luke 7:15).

For me, the meaning of Jesus' resurrection is consummately portrayed in Piero della Francesca's fifteenth-century fresco. It shows a steadfast Christ striding out of a marble tomb, holding a victory flag. At first, the image looks odd because this eruption of life, which if purely empirical would have been as impossible to ignore as a Tuscan earthquake, doesn't disturb the soldiers the artist also shows. They remain asleep, lounging against the sides of the sarcophagus. Their drowsy eyes stay closed even as a sturdy, risen foot is planted inches from them. But Piero knew that the resurrection could not have been evidenced in a lab, though it could be caught in a picture. It takes place in another life that contains mortal life and so can't be reduced to it. Its nature is akin to the apocalypse and the kingdom that are found within, to the meaning of a parable that comes with a revelation not an explanation, to the practices of silent prayer and inner sacrifice that are transformative because they re-orientate.

Jesus' life matters because he marks a unique turning point in the evolution of consciousness. Recovering the history is useful because it helps us understand the moment. But to perceive why he is pivotal, and what was his meaning, you do not need facts and texts to cross check. You need eyes to see and ears to hear. Then, you can work with the divine within you and know it flowing without. You can live.

Chapter 7

Christianity's High Noon

The life, death and resurrection of Jesus marks a point of no return. A consciousness that had been bubbling near the surface and, in the lives of certain individuals, occasionally poking above the waves, stretched its wings and took to the air. It became a definitive presence in human history, in principle available to all. The waters of John's baptism, which were cleansing, became the waters of an emergence into new life. Stepping out of the cave that was his tomb, Christ left the flickering light of original participation for the sunlight of reciprocal awareness, known without and within.

Paul became a key player in its transmission. "Behold, I tell you a mystery!" he declared to anyone who would listen (1 Cor 15:51) because it was a mystery he had experienced himself. The story is well known. He had a vision on the road to Damascus, was blinded and thrown from his horse. It became a pivotal moment through which he was born again. The Stoics whose writing he knew well, as he was to show when he visited Athens (Acts 17:29), perhaps helped him unpack the experience. They had described how conversion arises from a combination of abrupt change and steady assimilation. It would begin with a nagging sense that something is not quite right, "our consciousness of our weakness," as Epictetus puts it. That builds until the unease cannot be contained any longer, and the individual feels struck by an authority outside of themselves. Their axis of perception is knocked, sways, and then tumbles. It's what we would call a breakdown. It's part of the process, and invaluable, because the cracks let a light in. The *Logos* was making its presence felt, the Stoics inferred. It could power a new awakening and, slowly, a different way of life might form. It's likely that following his tumble, Paul disappeared for a few years to gather himself; to settle on the way (Gal 1:17). He came to call it, "dying every day" (1 Cor 15:31). He was shedding the old and putting on the new.

His genius was to recognize that the potential for conversion is in everyone. Again, the Stoics might well have provided a lead as they were champions of such cosmopolitanism. Paul's contemporary, Seneca, wrote: "God is near you, he is with you, he is within you ... God comes into men." Their sages stressed that all people are God's offspring, God's kin, because God is the one "in whom we live and move and have our being."

It fed into Paul's vision of a mystical union with God, which he understood as he developed the meaning of the life of Jesus the Christ. "For I am sure that neither death, nor life, nor anything in all creation ... will be able to separate us from the love of God in Christ Jesus our Lord" (Rom 8:38). To convert is to rouse the divine self that the prophets anticipated and the philosophers taught and was fully evoked in Jesus, the individual who had known and shown it so thoroughly.

It was for all. Paul fought fiercely for the recognition of his view when he harangued the Jerusalem-based leaders to recognize his apostleship to the gentiles. He had to work hard because Peter, James and the others in Jerusalem appear to have retreated after Jesus' death. Perhaps because of the trauma, they turned to the exclusive ethos of their upbringing, and didn't show much interest in those who weren't Jews.[58] They are condemning themselves, Paul insisted (Gal 2:11), because he, not they, had seen God's future. It is based upon response. That's why it is universal and, as good news, belongs to everybody.

The move was profoundly and radically liberating. It offered a freedom based upon an equality that didn't erase older civic distinctions and religious markers but simply leapt over them, transcending cult and social status altogether. "There is no longer Jew or Greek, there is no longer slave or free, there is no longer male or female," Paul preached in another astonishing passage

(Gal 3:28). This was a revolution that even the prophets and philosophers had failed to envision. It's an inner movement; a re-alignment of soul. Paul's metaphors stress how it's about "going beneath," "to the depths," "in the heart," and "discovering" what is "secret" and "hidden." It's direct participation in the life of God.

It meant he could assert that there is no longer slave or free and simultaneously advise the slave, Onesimus, to return to his master (Philemon). Their spiritual mutuality might overwrite, though not erase, their master-slave relationship. Alternatively, he could rule that Christians are free to eat meat offered to idols because it was so crucial to stress that what is ritually consumed does not matter. "Food will not bring us close to God" (1 Cor 8:7). Life is now found from the inside out, not taken from the outside in. But at the same time, some might choose not to eat idol meat, because they do not want to become a "stumbling block to the weak" – which is to say, to those who don't yet get the message (1 Cor 8:9). Spiritual individuality is not the same as thoughtless individualism, Paul took pains to stress, though he was routinely exasperated by those who lost sight of the fundamental vision and reverted to the old exclusivism. "For when one says, 'I belong to Paul', and another, 'I belong to Apollos', are you not merely human?" Paul pointed out (1 Cor 3:4). You hear the same failure today when Christians talk of being "Bible-believing," as if their experience of God is dictated by words on a page, or alternatively when others demand "sacramental security," as if the divine presence is magicked into existence by a kind of priestly conjuring trick. Paul longed for his fellows to be "spiritual people," to know of their union, to live from the mystery of their "twoness," as the psychologist of religion, Jeffrey Kripal, calls it: there's a conscious part of us that is "merely human" in space and time, living an individual life; and part of us of which we can become more conscious that is "spiritual," outside of space and time, sharing in the mind of God.[60]

Paul won the argument and Christians came to regard people as not limited by status or place. Christianity, as it formed, crystalized what had been an emergent anthropology. "It provided an ontological foundation for 'the individual,'" explains Larry Siedentop.[59] It did so in its promise that humans have access to the deepest levels of reality from within themselves.

This proved civilization-changing, though at first it made Roman and Jewish authorities wary. Individuals who are grounded in God can exhibit a loyalty to one another that lies beyond the reach of the state. Christians felt that they were, at base, sisters and brothers and that they belonged to another country, the metaphor that emerges early in Christianity.

It's a form of identity that was put on bloody show when Christians began to be martyred. It must have been part of the thrill for the crowds to watch these strange individuals, with their occult bonds, singled out to suffer and die. Nothing fuels violence as effectively as scorn combined with envy. Would they hold onto the deity in their bosom now? There's an echo of such malign excitement in the account of the stoning of Stephen. He gazes into heaven. His accusers cover their ears and shout (Acts 7:56–57).

That said, the independence of mind the Christians displayed must have chimed with what many were sensing in themselves. There were others who had developed a similar self-understanding that rested in realities beyond the civic and secular. A similar individuality was integral to the message of the philosophers. It was part of the attraction of the mystery religions. You can make a personal choice. You have agency.

Paul knew as much, as is demonstrated in the strategy he adopted on his missionary journeys. Upon arriving in a new town or city, his pattern was to go first to the diaspora synagogue and then to the local "God-fearers," the individuals and households who were not Jews but who were attracted to

Jewish monotheism. They had felt the mood in the air. Like the receptive hearers of Jesus' parables, they were half ready to hear a new message. He then tried to describe what had been revealed in the life of the Christ, at this turning point of history.

* * *

In his letters, the earliest surviving attempts to articulate it, he identifies the components that meant Jesus could experience life fully as human and divine, and so therefore could they. He realized that the experience of God that his Jewish ancestors had focused on, the I AM of Moses, could be combined with a Hellenistic experience of conscience and self-knowledge. From now on, divine will and human agency could be fused. There was no necessary competition. This is what Jesus had shown.

It's a major claim. It seems unlikely, given the mess human beings routinely make of things. Paul explained that it works like this, notably in his letter to the Romans.

An intimation of God, which is not an uncommon human experience, has, at first, a dismaying effect. It comes and goes like a peak experience – and, further, draws a person's attention to the traits that tend to undermine and destroy the vision, and their day-to-day flourishing. It's a deadly tendency that pervades all humanity, Paul concluded. He called it sin, "falling short." But what happens, if the individual is not entirely demoralized, is that the side that knows innately what's good can be nurtured, at least to some degree. To use Paul's terms, the person awakens to the free gift of eternal life in the Spirit. It can be consciously received, perhaps at first as an act of faith though, in time, it is recognized as actually having been present, undimmed all along. The individual comes to know a divine side of life and strives more consistently to align him- or herself to that Spirit.

But it still often feels otherwise. The experience is like being locked in a perpetual struggle between what's deadly and what's life-giving, between what the person would do and what they actually do. It's a battle fought out in practical choices, and in the inmost self. It's a conflict that cannot be avoided, Paul realized. It's taking place within the inner life of the cosmos, too, amongst the "powers and principalities," as he described them, and looks as if it will continue indefinitely.

And yet, there is an unconquerable goodness at play. This is what the resurrection of Christ had shown. The deadly can be discarded, and it is possible to live according to the divine that dwells in all things. Paul calls it glorious, meaning that it offers nothing less than knowledge of, and so participation in, God. Nothing can take or be taken from it. The question is how, given all the layers of struggle?

I think Paul came to realize that there is another turn in the path that leads to a settled awareness of life in God. He only finally understood what divine union meant when he ceased worrying about himself. He saw that worry is really a yearning to be rid of uncertainty and to gain control, as well as a vain attempt to rely on his own efforts. So, instead, he let his failures be. He accepted his weakness. It was in dying to himself that he reliably opened to an inflow of the deathless.

His suffering, which was extensive, was transformed. It became a reminder that there is always more than suffering. His anger, which continued to flare at times, came to be seen as a flawed version of divine passion. His thorn in the flesh became a means of grace. As he was crucified with Christ, as opposed to leaning on Christ's crucifixion and praying for his own agonies to go, he found God dwelling within him. He had learnt what Mary had on the morning of the resurrection: not to cling to Jesus but to be free to live his life in the Spirit (John 16:7 and 20:17). This was the truly sweeping realization, his central enlightenment.

It is a secret conception of freedom. Today, for example, the working assumption is that freedom means liberty from restraint in order to pursue what's desired. Spiritual freedom, though, is the liberty to realize what is truest in us, to see the "human form divine," to use William Blake's phrase – the twoness, which Blake said enables "double vision." It is the freedom to move from an involuntary, often conflicted embroilment with the powers and principalities of original participation to a conscious, active union with God under reciprocal participation. "There is a spirit in the soul, untouched by time and flesh, flowing from the Spirit, remaining in the Spirit, itself wholly spiritual. In this principle is God, ever verdant, ever flowering in all the joy and glory of his actual Self," as Meister Eckhart saw it.[61]

It comes about by being prepared to sacrifice everything false, transient and deluded; everything that is sought and gripped as if it were an essential part of us but is not. It's not that such things are inherently evil or bad. This is not a Manichean or puritanical creed. It's rather that, alongside knowledge of God, all things are seen for what they are.

After Paul, successive generations of patristic writers strove to keep a right focus on the full meaning of the historical moment that had released the timeless fact. "The Word of God became a man so that from a man you might learn how to become a god," wrote Clement of Alexandria in the second century. "By dwelling in one, the Word dwelt in all," discerned Cyril of Alexandria in the third century. "The Son of God became man so that we might become God," said Athanasius of Alexandria in the fourth. "The descent of God to the human level was at the same time the ascent of man to the divine level," preached Leo the Great in the fifth. The inner meaning of the gospel is something that is realized, and not readily summarized. It demands constant stressing and redressing.

Even Paul could be mistaken about its practical implications, on occasion, though he clearly grasped the heart of the matter. And his vision of freedom, union and life powered the long-term spread of Christianity. It projected a conception of what it is to be human that ran with the times and revolutionized them. It expanded upon Christ's breakthrough in the evolution of human consciousness.

The tangible outcomes that would shape a civilization began to emerge. One was the forging of networks not based upon kinship as a new basis for civic association. Christians could recognize one another by a link based not upon clan or city-state, but upon individual conversion and personal devotion. "Christianity's sharpest advantage was its inexhaustible ability to forge kinship-like networks among perfect strangers based on an ethic of sacrificial love," writes Kyle Harper.[62]

It introduced the ancient world to a novel understanding of human psychology, too, in the notion of free will. Greeks and Romans tended to assume that everything was thoroughly determined by fate. Freedom, for them, meant agreeing to this all-powerful feature of the cosmos. But a century or so after Paul, the Christian philosopher, Justin Martyr, became the first thinker to use the concept of free will in our sense. There really is such a thing as human agency. "The sudden appearance of philosophical concepts that will endure for centuries is rare," notes Harper.[63] That's because they appear in the relatively rare moments when consciousness definitively turns. The new understanding of free will is further evidence that the birth of Christianity was such a moment.

It was relentlessly defended by subsequent theologians. Many of the heresy battles fought in the centuries after Jesus, as well as the defenses of Christianity written against pagan philosophers, were, at heart, about the inalienability of this kind of inner freedom. If that went, the possibility of consciously understanding the nature of your association with the divine went. It's why, in fifth-century Constantinople, people on the street could be heard discussing the unbegotten nature of the Son, as Gregory of Nyssa famously observed. If it turned out that the Son were subordinate to the Father, humanity would be the puppet creature of God too, and the clock would be turned back to the fated cosmology of antiquity.

* * *

Christianity had relaunched the project of reciprocal participation by developing the most penetrating consciousness of individuality yet. In time, that was to spread around the world, shaping many other wisdom traditions, that in turn influenced the ongoing development of Christianity. The pattern of withdrawal leading to a re-engagement with others and nature, as well as the divine, repeated itself. It gradually pervaded many aspects of life. For example, by the fourth century, in Europe, it had been captured in a Latin word that, in our times, has become central to our own consciousness of life – *scientia* – though it meant something different back then.

Paul had affirmed what any educated Greek would have known, that God's invisible qualities can be visibly seen in nature. As Plato had shown in the *Timaeus*, God is continually doing geometry in all manner of cosmic intricacies. As the Stoics had intuited, there is a skill of "going with this flow," which is to say, discerning and living with the grain of the world.

The experience was picked up by Augustine and others who placed *scientia*, or natural philosophy, within the context of spiritual development. They argued that at the same time as natural philosophy reveals the causes of things, so it reveals the sustainer of all things. To perceive that is to perceive the excellence that is in human beings.[64] *Scientia* is a stepping stone to knowledge of God, and therefore to the best thing in us.

It was not yet a method, let alone a worldview. It was, rather, a virtue, a habit of mind that "perfects the powers that the individual possesses."[65] It wasn't about the accumulation of facts but about the strengthening of perception, ultimately the perception of God. Its purpose was to enable the human mind to mirror God's mind, reciprocally. "By this light, the rational creature is made deiform," as Aquinas came to express it in the medieval period.[66] He argued that a key benefit of learning geometry, for example, was training the individual in divine habits of harmony and proportion. It's as if drawing a right-angled triangle were a spiritual exercise. Knowing about Pythagoras' theorem would be an extra, thrown in for free.

* * *

By then, Christianity had become a worldview. It now shaped how people knew life. It provided the language of consciousness, the filter of experience. In the West, it became Christendom. Barfield painted a picture of what a medieval European person might have experienced as they looked up into the sky. He imagines what it would have been to know the cosmos with such enthralled thoughts and eyes.

> If it is daytime, we see the air filled with light proceeding from a living sun, rather as our own flesh is filled with blood proceeding from a living heart. If it is night-time, we do not merely see a plain, homogeneous vault pricked with separate points of light, but a regional, qualitative sky, from which first of all the different sections of the great zodiacal belt, and secondly the planets and the moon (each of which is embedded in its own revolving crystal sphere) are raying down their complex influences upon the earth, its metals, its plants, its animals and its men and women, including ourselves ...
>
> As to the planets themselves, without being specially interested in astrology, we know very well that growing things are specially beholden to the moon, that gold and silver draw their virtue from sun and moon respectively, copper from Venus, iron from Mars, lead from Saturn. And that our own health and temperament are joined by invisible threads

> to these heavenly bodies we are looking at. We probably do not spend any time thinking about these extra-sensory links between ourselves and the phenomena. We merely take them for granted.[67]

When the Christian soul went on pilgrimage, as many were inclined to do, the vision would have been confirmed in the gothic cathedral or holy shrine they found at the end of the journey. They would have seen astrological charts and stars painted onto the ceiling and walls, mapping the invisible, celestial threads. They would have found the extra-sensory links between human inner life and the inner life of nature celebrated on the surfaces of wooden screens and marble columns in the ornate foliage and wild animals carved from them. That some of the creatures depicted were legendary, like unicorns and the green man, was no affront to the science of the times. These were felt presences, not empirical observations, as were those of the stone gargoyles and angels – figures that signaled more of the spirited entities with whom humans share creation. The stories of the saints told of similar transpersonal connections, as in the tale of Hugh of Lincoln who was comforted by a swan or Edmund of East Anglia whose severed head was protected by a wolf.

Then, at the focus of the church, near the high altar, the pilgrim would have sought out the relics, the material remains of those who had radiated divine energy with a particular intensity because they had so embodied the consciousness of God. At the shrine, the pilgrim might further seek a miracle, which they would have thought of not as a divine intervention that broke scientific laws but as a moment of God's blessing that was different only because it was experienced explicitly and directly.

If this person were relatively uneducated, they would almost certainly not have talked about it in terms of dogmas or creeds, any more than most people today would describe driving a car in terms of the physics of internal combustion and gear ratios. A medieval believer might never utter the word, *credo*, "I believe," partly because they didn't speak good Latin and partly because during church services the creed was sung by the choir. It was not rehearsed by the congregation who moved about in the nave lighting candles or greeting neighbors. Their religion was experienced as the ragbag of activities, rites and stories that shaped the weeks and years, sustaining a bond with the pulse of life and directing a receptive piety. Religion was about feasting and fasting; about devotion to revered saints; about pilgrimages to holy places; about riffing on a mix of sacred scenes preserved in stained glass windows and folk myths passed down the generations. The mix tended to kindle an experiential, often inventive imagination, if not independence of thought. It produced mystery plays and was also fearful of magic.

At times, this darker side turned pitch black. The grisly history of persecution and crusade, for which Christianity seems to have a particular gift, amply attests to that. The terrible risk with asserting that inner life can image divine life is that a steady stream of often ruthless individuals will emerge who take it upon themselves to inquire into the accuracy of the match in cases they deem suspect. They might target other Christians. They might target other faiths. Diarmaid MacCulloch notes that Christians began harassing each other within two years of Constantine affirming, and so sanctioning, the new movement.[68] It's a doubly troubling fact because that was easily within living memory of their severest Roman persecution, under Diocletian.

* * *

The medieval version of reciprocal participation meant that the Bible was read in highly imaginative ways, too. It was treated as an extended allegory, which meant that it was both literal and symbolic – though that distinction imposes an artificial division on the medieval mind for whom everything was an intermingling of surface and depth. The Bible was as was everything else that God touched: exemplary and illustrative, inspired and basically trust-worthy. The created order reflected God's truth; for all that, it was often hard to pick up the echo of that perfection.

The assumption is woven into the New Testament itself. In one of the earliest books, the Letter to the Galatians, Paul explains that Abraham had two wives, Hagar and Sarah, because God had made two covenants with the patriarch (Gal 4:24). It's an observation as inventive as anything uttered by the Deuteronomists about Moses.

The gospel writers who came next routinely made similar links. Consider a verse from Matthew that he took from a Greek version of First-Isaiah, "Behold a virgin shall conceive and bear a son" (Matthew 1:23). He used it to incorporate into his narrative of the birth of Jesus the standard ancient trope that individuals whose lives turned out to carry world significance must have had divine parentage. They were virgin-born, which is to say that the significance of their life arose at base from divine activity, not human desire. The same was said of Alexander the Great and the Emperor Augustus, and I don't suppose their admirers were much bothered that biology must have had something to do with it, too. I'm sure as well that Matthew wouldn't have edited his insight had he learnt that the Hebrew and original version of the text upon which he drew, and didn't know, actually read: "A young woman is with child" (Isaiah 7:14). His aim would have remained the same, to speak of the significance of Jesus. He might have inferred that the altered meaning was a divinely-inspired amendment. The weight of Jesus' life demanded that he write "virgin." The Greek scripture had confirmed it.

By the second century, the scholar, Origen, had systematized such exegesis. For him, the literal sense is not what actually happened. Rather, the literal is what the human author had intended to convey. By focusing on that, the receptive reader would find the full truth of the scripture disclosing itself to them, as it emerged in the space between their mind, the divine mind, and the text. The process might reveal something morally useful or practically instructive or new and revelatory. This is the sense in which the Bible was said to have authority. It was a window and a wellspring, as well as a map.

Nature worked in the same way because, as Origen remarked, everything on earth has a resemblance to something in heaven. The popular image of a pelican in her piety provides a case in point. It shows the long-necked, large-billed bird, standing on a nest, stabbing her breast to feed blood to her young. It was simultaneously regarded as a description of what happened in nature, a lesson in how human beings should live, and the bird unwittingly attesting to God's relationship with human beings, who are divine offspring. There is a biblical allusion, too. As the Psalmist sings, "I resemble a pelican of the wilderness" (Ps 102.6).

Planting such messages in nature was what God did, and later theologians were to note that one of the distinguishing features God possesses is having the power to infuse all things with such meanings, much as human beings can do in a more limited way in music and words. And why would it be otherwise? The reciprocal mind experienced clearly that God's life bathes and so molds all life.

The relationship between the body and the soul was similarly experienced as a continuity. How these aspects of life were allied was widely discussed on the basis that the one flows into the other. The body fits the soul. Or it might be said that the body is to the soul as ice is to water: they are different states of being. Or again, there's the word that was used to capture the connection, *methexis*, borrowed from the Greeks. It originally expressed the emotions and mood exchanged between a cast and audience in a play or entertainment. It was borrowed for the relationship between body and soul because they share an invisible, animating energy that transmits. You feel this energy directly in the revelations of Julian of Norwich, who felt her body to be sharing in the pain of the crucified body of Jesus. It filled her soul with love, so that she could utter "All will be well." In the *methexis*, though an agony, she realized she could never be alone. Her body did not isolate her. Ensouled, it was the means of her participation.

It was possible because the body was not thought of as one thing and the soul as some ghostly and wholly different other. Similarly, the mind was to the brain as light is to the eyes. This is how it felt, that consciousness is not something that only goes on inside solitary heads, any more than light could be something that only exists in isolated eyes. Human interiority reflects the interiority of all things, which is in turn known as sustained and fed by the very life of God. It was an experience of consciousness that, in the West, lasted for over one thousand years.

Chapter 8

Reform and Science

Life during the Middle Ages was experienced very differently from now, and that's hardly a surprise. Most people lived closer to the land, closer to the divine and, experientially speaking, closer to the planets and stars as their influence washed over Earth. If, today, it's easy to feel like an onlooker on life, peering out from an island of awareness somewhere inside your head, the medieval person must have felt like an immersed participant whose life was naturally involved with the seasons, the saints, and the skies. It's an image of things that has now been discarded, to recall C.S. Lewis's neat one-word summary.[69]

Things began to change in the latter centuries of the medieval period, coming to a head, dramatically, in the sixteenth century with the complicated events of the Reformation.[70] This transformation has had as big an impact upon interior life as anything else in European history. It takes us into a third phase for Christianity, if the Hebrew and Greek periods before the life of Jesus are regarded as the first and Christendom is the second, because what unfolded with the Reformation was another development of the experience of ourselves, nature and God. It marked the beginning of a new period of participative withdrawal. There's much debate about what caused it and how it unfolded in different parts of Europe, but its impact is relatively clear and that's the important point here. It can be described like this.

A growing impulse of the late medieval papacy precipitated an unexpectedly radical reaction. The church had sought, perhaps in good faith, to provide the people with a guaranteed assurance of eternal life. It had decreed that money was the means. Donations would flow to Rome to fund splendid pilgrimage churches and sustain religious orders that were dedicated to saying masses for the dead and, in return, the church would deliver the comforts of redemptive indulgences. Though some people criticized it, and in retrospect it's clearly a mistake to think you can buy spiritual security, many clearly gained much of value from the system.

The contradiction remained tolerable until it no longer was for a young Augustinian monk named Martin Luther. He's an invaluable figure in tracking shifts in consciousness at this juncture not only because he is, arguably, the one person without whom the Reformation as a widespread social movement is inconceivable, but also because the wealth of surviving material about him means that much can be discerned of his inner life, and what he seeded in the inner life of others.[71]

He visited Rome in 1510 and was appalled by the corruption that the inflow of cash had generated. "They preach only human doctrines who say that as soon as the money clinks into the money chest, the soul flies out of purgatory," he subsequently wrote in one of his famous 95 theses, posted on a Wittenberg church door in 1517. His outrage was fiery and unleashed a temper that attacked the spiritual economy. Protestantism was the unanticipated by-product, with a dramatically further enhanced sense of being an individual springing from it. At the time, the turbulence was severe. It led to personal crises and open warfare across Europe, though in retrospect, it's possible to see the revolution as having good as well as negative consequences. The task is to tease one from the other because the impact of the Reformation is still, largely, what most directly shapes the struggle with inner life that Westerners have now.

* * *

Interestingly, this latest turning of the wheel of participation has at least one material feature in common with the Deuteronomic reforms that had happened two millennia previously. It was powered by innovative writing technology that had a devolving effect, this time in the form of the printing press.

Movable type and screw presses encouraged Luther to be prolific. In the decade between 1520 and 1530, it's estimated that he composed 20 percent of all the treatises and sermons that were printed and disseminated across German lands, and they were extensively heard and read. A bit like a stellar tweeter of today, the dominance of his personality, coupled to the thrill of his logic, cultivated a feeling that the individual can become the best source of authority because one individual was best demonstrating what was wrong with Christendom and what was right. It was a sense with which Luther, from the 1520s onwards, wholeheartedly concurred. By then, he knew himself to be a person who had faced down the papal and imperial courts and, like the early martyrs, had proven his personal connection with God by embracing the prospect of being burned for his faith.

What is crucial is that he stressed the centrality of the individual in relation to God once more, though also remodeled the notion of individuality in so doing. That happened in a twofold move. On the one hand, he popularized what is now the commonplace idea that the most important thing in spiritual life is having a direct relationship with God, as opposed to one embedded in the divine flux of the lives of saints and angels, nature and celestial bodies. But on the other hand, he simultaneously disdained and derided what went on in people's inner lives. Henceforth, a person's relationship with God was to be based not upon felt experience but entirely different ground.

Luther believed that it was only by forcefully rejecting the fallen nature of the human state that a lost person could be born again, and that corruption was no more keenly experienced than in the ups and downs of consciousness. A thorn in the flesh was not a potential window of grace but a sign of vice and a guarantee of condemnation, unless you were saved. The freedom promised in the gospel could come about if, and only if, the individual yielded to God's life, and God's life alone.

He was clearly an unsettled man. He regularly suffered from physical collapses that we'd now say were psychosomatic. The spiritual practices offered by the church, such as pilgrimage and confession, did little or nothing to ease his pain. As he wrote in a brief autobiography: "I was a sinner before God with an extremely disturbed conscience." He was haunted by his mind. He failed to make Paul's move and come to welcome his weaknesses as reminders of God's strength and instead grew intensely suspicious of any presumed divine intimacy. He desired a relationship with God that was not about reciprocity and union but utter dependency, secured not from within but without. He found that security in the pages of the Bible, read not imaginatively but literally. *Sola scriptura* became his cry. Only scripture could shine with "a spiritual light far clearer than the sun," he insisted.

He lived during a good time for the scriptural illumination that so comforted him. The *via moderna*, cultivated by Renaissance humanism, was in full swing. It stressed the importance of returning to original texts to gain accurate sources that could then be translated with precision into the vernacular languages of the people. Unlike followers of the *via antiqua,* who reveled in improvisational, allegorical exegesis, followers of the *via moderna* were critical of treating scripture in the free form ways that such readings allowed. Clear and unambiguous meanings became prized. The historical must be separated from the symbolic so that ancient authors could be heard speaking plainly. A new typeface was invented to foreground the most desirable reader experience, italic. The cursive script nurtured a sense of directness. An italicized passage has an authoritative voice that the reader mustn't play with, but instead must submit to and hear.

Interpretation stopped being a case of both/and. It became a matter of either/or. Luther asserted: "It was very difficult for me to break away from my habitual zeal for allegory. And yet I was aware that allegories were empty speculations and the froth, as it were, of the Holy Scriptures. It is the historical sense alone which supplies the true and sound doctrine." The person who was to become his fellow reformer a generation later, John Calvin, put it even more succinctly: "Allegory is idolatrous."

Luther's rejection of inner life was expressed in other ways. Take the key Reformation debate concerning free will. Early Christianity had grown with the sense that the individual could turn to God and discover the divine incarnate within, and Luther's slightly older contemporary, Erasmus, defended the freedom of the human psyche on the same grounds. It was a labyrinthine issue, he admitted in his discourse, "The Freedom of the Will." Humans can clearly turn away from those things that lead to God, as well as choose them. But that very dynamic reveals freedom of will and further, Erasmus continued, it's the choice that potentially makes the individual a fellow-worker with divine grace. It's a crucial involvement, one of reciprocity.

Luther aggressively disagreed. He rejected free will in his response to Erasmus, entitled "On the Enslaved Will." He goes so far as to announce that he would not wish to be given free will, if he had such a power of choice, because free will would leave him uncertain as to whether he had received God's grace. Might he have to do more to receive such a blessing? Might he have unwittingly made choices that jeopardized his salvation? Might he actually be working against God and for the devil? Luther did not want any secret human faculty to compromise his relationship with God. His disturbed conscience was too buffeted by forces beyond his control. It could not mirror God's life, even poorly. His conclusion was affirmed by Calvin, who later declared human interiority to be in a state of "total depravity."

Luther's wariness showed up elsewhere. For example, throughout his life he told the story of how he had come to be an Augustinian monk. His youthful vocation had arisen during a thunderstorm from which God had saved him. Tempests were commonly believed to be conjured by demons and, on this occasion, God had apparently answered his prayer and intervened to calm the storm. But the story was not wholly happy. He started worrying that the tempest might have left him bewitched. Such uncertainties fueled his later decision to trust God and scripture alone and the incident, in its retelling, illustrates his own personal withdrawal from participation with the inside of the world. He came to feel that it was impossible to discern the benign from the malign forces that lurked therein.

Luther focused on a contradiction that had arisen with medieval Christendom, the mixing up of secular power and spiritual salvation, the struggle to serve both God and mammon. But pretty soon, contradictions surfaced in his own position. In particular, he sought certainty from the Bible and it was a certainty only the individual could know as the church could no longer be trusted. But at the same time, he preached that all humans are ridden with fatal flaws. He had to assert the authority of the individual and at the same time deny it, a tension that "was obscured partly by Luther's insistence on scriptural transparency and supremacy, and partly by the sheer force of his personality," writes Richard Rex.[72] The strain shows up in the neologisms of the age, in particular the sudden deployment of words hyphenated with "self" which had hardly existed before: "self-conceit," "self-confidence," "self-contempt," "self-pity." They track a notable rise in anxious preoccupations with the self.

The pressures led to violence expressed in the iconoclasm of the age. Reformers decapitated statues, nailed scriptures over holy pictures, and whitewashed the wall paintings that had spoken to the medieval pilgrim of their intimacy with the cosmos and God. Images came to be regarded with the same distrust as inner life. If they weren't destroyed they were converted into moralizing signs. They were made "explicit," writes Iain McGilchrist, "understood by reading a kind of key, which demonstrates that the image is [now] thought of simply as an adornment, whose only function is to fix meaning more readily in the mind – a meaning which could have been better stated literally."[73]

The historian, Lyndal Roper, sums up the impact of Luther's inner struggles. He rejected the participation that had shaped medieval Christian awareness. He inclined towards intellectual uses of the Bible. He lost sight of the meditative dimensions of faith. He preferred action over contemplation. "This would shape the character of Lutheranism and of Protestantism itself for centuries to come."[74]

It also meant that when mystics from amongst their own ranks emerged – individuals including Jakob Böhme and Emanuel Swedenborg, William Blake and Charles Wesley – they were, on the whole, ostracized or treated as heretics. In response, the period saw the birth of secret societies, from Freemasonry to Rosicrucianism. They were secret not in the sense of trying to convey spiritual subtleties or the transformation of inner life, but in the sense of going underground, monitoring initiates, guarding rites. In a way, they had to, so as to avoid persecution, though my sense is that their disappearance from public view also meant they could avoid scrutiny and discernment, which has meant that the symbols and mysteries they guarded tended to degenerate.

Introspection, arising from the quest for certainty about salvation, didn't disappear. But the uneasiness about it meant that it was inclined to narrow into obsessions over who was saved. Alternatively, it was projected into fixations about "popery" or "superstition," words also coined at the time to convey disapproval of the Catholic church's Counter-Reformation. So powerful was the feeling that it's only in recent decades that lighting candles and making pilgrimages have become attractive in Protestant circles once more.

The Reformation's legacy shows up in further shifts in the meanings of words. Take, "subjective." Ever since Aristotle, it had meant "that which exists in itself." What was inward had been the primary locus of something's meaning. After the Reformation, subjective came to mean "existing in human consciousness" and so probably of doubtful worth. The inward was separated from what was deemed outward and "objective," which in turn became synonymous with "true." Faith flipped similarly, morphing from "felt trust" to "cognitive belief." It ceased to be the starting point for a quest to understand and became a cerebral statement of what should be affirmed, ideally without question. It becomes faith in faith.

* * *

These are the downsides. But, as with turns of the experiential cycle before, the Reformation withdrawal of participation produced major upsides. It equally drove the evolution of consciousness towards the experience of life that is our own and which is often, rightly, valued.

Paradoxically, given Luther's rejection of free will, religious freedom came to be stressed, eventually finding full articulation in philosophers like John Locke. In "A Letter Concerning Toleration" he argued that churches should be free associations, joined according to personal conscience, because it must be lawful for the individual to take care of the salvation of their soul. Freedom of thought and expression came to be prized, nowadays being treated as sacrosanct ends in themselves. A key tenet of liberalism is that it shouldn't matter what you practice or preach, so long as it stays within socially acceptable bounds, because what matters is your freedom to do so. In a way, it's a further development of Jesus' realization that it is not what goes into someone that counts but what comes out, only whereas Christians had previously felt that what comes out counts because it's a measure of a person's alignment with God, it counts in the modern world because a person should be able to give voice to the private deity conscience has become. It's a cut off not connected kind of freedom.

On another front, the modern sense of history experienced as time moving forward emerges. Progress no longer meant a "royal journey" but "development" and "advance." Thinkers began to gain a sense of periods of history, inventing categories from "antiquated" to "contemporary." Barfield suggests that the move from the Greek *historia*, which had meant "knowledge gained by inquiry," to history as "the study of the past," arose with the need for objectivity from the Bible. Protestants became interested in dating scriptural events in an effort to understand them better. They embarked on investigations that were unimaginable to their forebears, and were not all helpful or wise. In 1650, the Primate of All Ireland, James Ussher, calculated the age of the Earth by stacking up the Biblical generations back to Adam. He fixed creation on Saturday 22 October, 4004 BCE, at about 6pm.

A clearer benefit is that the Reformers unsettled the social order that, up to then, had fixed the place of women. They stressed afresh the importance of the individual's response to God, at least in theory, and so championed the availability of God's Word to everyone, with the need for education that implies. They, therefore, cut across the impulse, common in the medieval world, to preserve the social structures that were felt to mirror heavenly hierarchies. Social mobility became much more possible. Consider the early follower of Luther, Argula von Grumbach. In 1523, she wrote a letter that supported his cause and had it published. It ran to fourteen editions in just two months and made her famous.

Attitudes towards fleshly life shifted as well. Luther had argued that because everything natural is fallen, sexuality might as well be enjoyed, for what it's worth. It wasn't a ringing endorsement but it did deconstruct the old habit of layering human beings by placing celibate bishops and priests on top and copulating laypeople at the bottom. "The works of monks and priests, be they never so holy and arduous, differ no whit in the sight of God from the works of the rustic toiling in the field or the woman going about her household tasks," Luther explained. Everyone has a vocation, a calling.

Finally, the medieval understanding of *scientia* changed. Again, it happened, in part, because of the way Luther and Calvin stressed the nature of the Bible's authority. Scripture is self-authenticating. The believer knows because the believer is personally convinced, as they engage with scripture in ways that are analytical, rather than allegorical; and literal, rather than imaginative. So, too, "[t]he new experimental scientists appealed to what they had seen with their own eyes." writes Alec Ryrie.[75] The Reformation prepared the human mind for a different way of observing the natural world and an approach that dissected things, in what came to be called the scientific method. Wrestling with quantitative details, as opposed to detecting qualitative possibilities, became the order of the day. It's an ability that requires a particular kind of attention and a different consciousness, that of modern scientific materialism.

* * *

The approach was distilled, just over a 100 years after Luther posted his theses, when the philosopher, Francis Bacon, composed his *Novum Organum Scientiarum*, or "new instrument of science." He argued that humanity couldn't rely on discerning the intrinsic purposes of things, as medieval contemplative *scientia* inferred. Neither could intuition be trusted to reveal the inside of the world, as had been assumed since Aristotle and Plato. Instead, the new instrument of science was to be rigorous logic. It would be objective by working with observable causes and their measurable effects. It would reflect not on forms of being, but rules and axioms.

Bacon was an innovator. He applied the Latin, *lex,* meaning "law," to nature, and soon after his followers started talking about "laws of nature." Any secrets were to be exposed to the light of day. In short, where Luther had striven to denounce the inner life of individuals, Bacon discarded the inner life of the cosmos. He mechanized its workings, instead, as well as the means of investigating it. "The mind must not be left to take its own course, but must be guided at every step, and the business be done as if by machinery," he explained.

Thinkers in this early modern period started to see cogs and wheels everywhere, much as today people spontaneously reach for informational bits and bytes when discussing anything from brains to black holes. Mechanical engineering was to them as computer science is to us. The upshot was that people started to experience the cosmos in this way. It's the way they imagined things. The new metaphors even felt as if they explained what it is to be human.

Take one small detail from the year 1666, when Charles II introduced fashionable society to the waistcoat. It became the defining item of sartorial elegance almost overnight, along with its crucial accessory, the pocket watch. Suddenly, large sections of the population developed the habit of reaching for the portable machines that they carried in their coats to check whether they were on time. The clocklike regularity of life became a mass experience. It's not unlikely that the pocket watch did far more than maths to persuade the general populous that Galileo, Bacon and Descartes were right about the mechanical vision of things.

John Donne thought so. His poem "Obsequies of the Lord Harrington" likens the soul to a clock's spring and the heart to a clock's wheel. He notes how, even before the waistcoat, pocket watches were loading individuals with guilt over really rather small faults, like being late. Time was becoming a tyrant. The present moment wasn't one in which to experience God, but one in which to fret.

Donne detected the ways in which portable watches, alongside other technologies, were distancing people from a participative appreciation of nature. Instead of ordering the day by the rising and setting of the Sun, people now had "a clock so true, as might the Sun control." A machine came to be experienced as more accurate, trustworthy and real than the Sun, whose movements human beings could judge and find wanting. The model censored how nature might speak. Rather than the Sun resonating with a wonder beyond itself, as a child of the Good, it became fascinating insofar as science could explain it.

The mood spread into the church, where there emerged an imperative to regularize religious truths and give faith a firm grounding in rational and empirical certainty. Science was based on the book of nature, as religion was on the book of scripture, and for a couple of centuries, it seemed that the two were complementary because as Robert Boyle noted, "[both] have the same author, so the study of the latter does not at all hinder the inquisitive man's delight in the study of the former." Galileo was driven by a profound sense that the new science was a divine gift, the rejection of which was partly what fired his anger at the ecclesiastical authorities, leading to his trial and house arrest: "I do not feel obliged to believe that the same God who has endowed us with sense, reason, and intellect has intended us to forgo their use," he fumed. Another astronomical giant of the age, Johannes Kepler, felt that his discoveries were "thinking God's thoughts after him." He argued that, "The chief aim of all investigations of the external world should be to discover the rational order which has been imposed on it by God and which He revealed to us in the language of mathematics." Newton too felt that "nature does nothing in vain" because its rigorous beauty so clearly speaks of God. "This most elegant system of the sun, planets, and comets could not have arisen without the design and dominion of an intelligent and powerful being," he wrote.

None of these men were atheists, and that perception of life wasn't yet fully possible. The meaning of things had not yet totally drained away. The symbolism of texts and the intuitions of the soul could still be trusted to a degree because people lived in the afterglow of medieval reciprocal participation. Newton could be fascinated by alchemy without contradiction; Kepler by numerology. But that experience of life was on borrowed time.

* * *

In the nineteenth century it ran out. Part of the issue was the need to regularize the scientific enterprise, to take account of all its discoveries and knit them into a coherent whole. A central figure in this push was the clergyman and master of Trinity College, Cambridge, William Whewell. In the mid-nineteenth century, he gazed with growing panic on science's untidy ragbag of investigations and breakthroughs. He couldn't be sure that the scientific pieces scattered before him fitted into the same puzzle. He feared science was a "great empire falling to pieces."

In effect, he responded by returning to the Reformation theme of biblical self-authentication. Science could be called science if it were recognized as such by "scientists," the noun that he coined. It's a solution akin to not being able to decide what art is and so defining art as "what artists do."

The self-referential nature of science deepened the withdrawal of participation. It made science autonomous, capable of assessing other claims to knowledge and resistant to external assessment itself. It fed an assumption that inert matter is the basic stuff out of which everything is made. It was the move that finally made science a worldview, with the assumption that the meaning of things is not innate but is formed from the conclusions of empirical investigators. They look onto the world dispassionately, observing nature as if from without, rather than resonating with nature from within. At best, God might be a celestial engineer who designed the universe clock, but probably God is unnecessary and dead. There is no inside of the world, no world soul or divine imprint, and human consciousness, too, must either be an inexplicable exception to the rule, a flickering flame of awareness in the darkness, or, more likely, not real at all but a delusional by-product of neurochemical processes.

It's called scientism and, from the nineteenth century onwards, it led to a new ethic: it's better to brave the mechanistic meaninglessness of life seemingly exposed by science than to believe in misconceptions like God, for all that they might console. You're a "lumbering robot," Richard Dawkins informed readers of his 1976 bestseller, *The Selfish Gene,* in a recent iteration of the creed. Today, many scientists have a reflexive habit of distancing themselves from anything that might be interpreted as a spiritual or religious belief, let alone vitalist secret.

However, there's been a pushback. The problem, as the philosopher of science, Mary Midgley, has noticed, is that such scientism is "life-blind." The mechanical model on which it depends is useful to a point but it can't hope to capture all sorts of facets of experience, like consciousness and feelings, meaning and free will. Machines can be disassembled and reassembled without suffering damage, whereas organisms that are dissected die. People comprehend, where machines only calculate. And no machine has an inner life and individuality, no matter how complex it becomes. You never feel guilty for turning one off.

Someone who says people are machines may be a great scientist, Barfield noted, though a person who says they *are* a machine is probably falling apart. Or as one of the twentieth-century's pioneering physicists, Werner Heisenberg, argued: rigid materialism is "obviously too narrow for an understanding of the essential parts of reality" – parts of reality that he listed as including mind, soul, life, and God.[76] His point was that these features of life need to be embraced, not excluded, before science declares that it has explained life.

A similar openness meant that Albert Einstein could report sensing the subtle force that lies behind science's laws and insights: his imagination allowed him to do so. My old physics tutor, the cosmologist, Carlos Frenk, reached the same conclusion: "I think that God was a physicist. I don't see how the order of the universe can be explained intrinsically within the universe itself ... if you're a cosmologist, you look at the universe and to me there's only just one conclusion."[77] There's an inside to the whole world.

They are dimensions of reality that won't be put down. The big question of our times is how they can be best picked back up. It's the issue felt by those who sense our crises are fundamentally spiritual crises. It's the imperative known by others who never supposed that consciousness is something that only goes on inside skulls, which must include anyone with faith in God. We've come to the crux point of our day. We've explored why inner life evolved and mattered back then. But how might its secrets matter once more, now?

Chapter 9

We Must Be Mystics

Owen Barfield came to the conclusion that we're passing through an inevitable, perhaps necessary phase of withdrawal and alienation. Although atheism and scientism can be seen as definitive rejections of God, they may in fact be features of a stage. They could be part of a further unfolding of the incarnation that, by making space for as yet only partially imagined forms of participation, are integral to the third stage in Christianity's development. The hint that this may be so is found by spotting a pattern. Atheism and scientism are iconoclastic movements. They are both linked to enhancements in the consciousness of being individual. They have facilitated a range of reforms that have deepened people's sense of inner freedom, expressed in good things from social mobility to universal education. But could they also become the source of a renewed relationship with nature and God?

Of course, mistakes have been made and wrong turnings taken. The mind cannot be the only bit of the universe that is inexplicably conscious, existing like a ghost in the cosmic machine. Science is not the enemy of religion, for all that some judge its success by the extent to which it can dissolve theological insights like an acid. But maybe the time is right to move onto the next stage of self-awareness that embraces once more a rich engagement with life and a renewed rootedness in reciprocity.

The way forward, I believe, is to return to the centrality of religious experience, the intuition that there's more, and the realization that Christianity, alongside other wisdom traditions, can make surprising felt sense.[78] We still need what the ancients developed, including spiritual reading and practices of silence; the embrace of uncertainty and trainings of the self. But there'll be a further dimension to any genuinely progressive spirituality that can embrace the gains of modern times. What might that look like? Can we begin to discern its outlines and feel a way forward?

It's not a question of turning back, though looking back is stimulating and valuable because it illuminates how inner life evolves and shows what it can be. So, under original participation, divine life is experienced directly. You almost catch it when Homer describes Achilles realizing he mustn't strike Agamemnon because Athena appears and pulls back his head; or when Jacob demands a blessing from God by fighting all night with an angel. But this is not our way of life now. Then, under reciprocal participation, divine life is experienced as the innate meaning of things. You feel it in Plato's journey to the soulful vitality of the world, and in Paul's astonished realization that he is free to identify with the source of life. That's closer to our experience, though it lies on the far side of the Reformation and the scientific revolution.

Modern people can have glimpses of both these forms but, for the most part, divine life must be found differently. So what now can help? There is one key faculty. The secret life of things, their presence and soul, will only be steadily regained imaginatively.

* * *

Imagination is crucial because it can achieve a step out of individual isolation without losing the modern experience of personhood. It can become a reconciling agency, an answer to the yearning, without compromising the me that is me and the you that is you. C.S. Lewis called it "joy"[79] and poets are often the guardians of its wisdom. As Ted Hughes explained: "Imagination isn't merely a surplus mental department meant for entertainment, but the most essential piece of machinery we have if we are going to live the lives of human beings."[80]

His description of the imagination as a "piece of machinery" is helpfully arresting. It underlines the fact that for the modern psyche any resurgence will follow a deliberate act. It'll be the result of a quest. There's a decision an individual must make if they seek to renovate the soul and refocus the mind. Choice is fundamental to re-engaging in the work of knowing you are not a machine, but are in the image of God as a human person.

Post-enlightenment poets like Wordsworth and Coleridge were early adopters of this way. They realized it offers a form of participation that can enjoy the benefits of individuality and quicken the spirit. This was the significance of their publication of the *Lyrical Ballads* in 1798. In Coleridge's summary, "we receive but what we give." When the imaginative mind ventures forth, it doesn't return empty handed.

However, imagination is also a complicated notion. It has a mixed reputation and people are suspicious of it. Does it trade in genuine insights or mere inventions? Does it bear truth or indulge fantasies? Where's its proof?

The ambiguity is illuminated by the history of the word. In the ancient world, it meant something different. Then, it carried the outward meaning of "receiving the *imago*," the images that were thought to be thrown off from the surfaces of things and absorbed by the senses. It was, in effect, a theory of seeing before Newtonian optics was postulated.

In the later Middle Ages, "imagination" started to take on the more recognizable meaning of fantasy. It began to denote a mental image, rather than an *imago*, that might well have no physical existence, or at least no physical existence yet. There is a dynamic of withdrawal in this shift. What had been an exchange with the external world is reconceived as a wholly inner dynamic. The imagination has moved inside. It requires not so much reception as discernment. After all, it might be detecting what, in truth, is just whimsy and, even if genuinely inspired, it'll need to be worked on and developed. Athena does not simply appear and pull back heads any more. Dreams must be made real.

Shakespeare provided a neat summary of these varieties of meaning in his well-known lines from *A Midsummer Night's Dream*. "The lunatic, the lover, and the poet, / Are of imagination all compact." They are "compact" both because the imaginative activities of all three "apprehend more than cool reason ever comprehends," and because they are all also vulnerable to the ways in which such apprehensions play tricks with the mind. Lunatics, lovers and poets can be mistaken in their respective visions of "devils," "things unknown" and/or "airy nothings." But still, Shakespeare insists, there seems to be more going on with the imagination than just the generation of "fancy's images." He would know.

Imagination can produce fantastic vacuities, for sure. But there is another possibility. The soul's "imaginary sight" may see more than the empirical ever can. As Shakespeare famously elsewhere put it: "There are more things in heaven and earth, Horatio, than are dreamt of in your philosophy." From a first possibly distorted sense of something, the imagination may show a truth that is gradually revealed over time. It led Shakespeare to present the imagination as an intermediate zone. It's somewhere between the subjective and the objective. It hovers at an edge, on a threshold. It's the domain we enter into when we hear a play, a poem, a parable. It's a region of revelation.

He was onto something key, and modern philosophy has fleshed out how we routinely perceive things through the combined activity of our physical senses and imaginative capacities. What is sometimes called the "imaginal" shapes and forms the otherwise "blooming, buzzing confusion" of mere apprehension, to recall William James' phrase. The experience of looking into a mirror is an example. You see your reflection and might wonder where the doppelgänger is located. It's not behind the mirror because if you look, you see a wall or thin air.

You might toy with the possibility that the double is not real, though it seems real enough. Does it exist in your mind or in the mirror or in both? The truth is in both, the mind and the mirror brought together to produce the sight. This is what the human imagination can do.

Rainbows are another case in point.[81] These bright arcs of colors are seen as clearly as reflections, and yet, if you search for the end of the rainbow you will not only not find a crock of gold, you won't find the end either. Rainbows exist in the intermediate zone between physical and mental worlds, which explains why their meaning is not fixed but has changed with changes of consciousness. For Noah, under original participation, they were a sign of God's promise. For us, with no spontaneous sense of the interpenetration of God and nature, they are enjoyed as a lovely meteorological effect. Only when they are depicted in a painting, or are caught in a photograph, might their symbolic meaning be re-evoked so that they speak once more of hope.

Reflections and rainbows are vivid examples but they are not exceptions to the rule. Since the work of Immanuel Kant, the imaginal has taken center stage in theories of perception. It's like a pair of glasses, manufactured by the mind that brings what we see into focus. The great philosopher of the Enlightenment argued that we don't know "the thing in itself" but perceive what our minds can represent – trees, sunshine, soil, showers. The mind's eye fashions them as much as the biological eye registers them. It's why quantum physics is so difficult to understand. At the level of the very, very small, science exposes us to a level of reality where our imaginations fail. Are these specks of light really particles or are they waves or both or neither? Are they some kind of field spread out probabilistically in space and time? The debate amongst physicists about the right way to interpret quantum physics is an indication of one place where the current imaginal breaks down. The same might be said of the debate amongst theologians of the best way to envisage God.

But we must trust the imagination with its limits because it is, in a sense, all that we've got. The question is whether we have perceived and qualified, or disqualified, its figurations correctly. Insofar as we have, something of the thing in itself comes through. We can connect.

* * *

Psychotherapy's understanding of the imagination developed along similar lines, to a point now that helps elucidate how the imagination can be connecting. In the early days, Sigmund Freud was skeptical of it. He argued that it's purely fanciful, on the assumption that all human imagining is the projection of unconscious fantasies onto others and the world around. He concluded that art and religion are no less the product of these sublimations. As cultural productions, they are highly developed versions of shared anxieties and traumas, which emerge to help people relate to their fears. They offer ways to befriend the turmoil inside. He wrote about how Leonardo's art was driven by buried homosexual urges and concluded that the Judeo-Christian deity is a father-figure who is imagined to live in the sky, because the father-figure who dwells in human hearts is a little too close for comfort. He wasn't entirely wrong, either, at least in the latter case. People can treat God like that when they seek to appease or escape him, or conversely when they call down his blessing to sanction their own authority.

However, a later psychotherapist, Donald Winnicott, revised Freud's view. He argued that whilst human beings are fanciful creatures, spraying all sorts of fictions and delusions onto the world, some of these flights of fancy must be true. If they weren't, we'd all be inhabiting castles in the air and left unable to communicate, do science or feel real. Physics would have the same epistemological status as sci-fi. Common sense would be no more grounded than psychotic hallucinations.

Winnicott concluded that discernment is key. It's a process of continuously sifting the imaginative wheat from the fanciful chaff. Psychotherapy is, in part, a personal practice of such disentanglement. It helps distinguish between what comes solely from a patient's past – their memories, fears, prejudices – and what comes from a side of life that is bigger than those assumptions. The talking cure can discover what are abiding "sins," in the sense of engrained habits that unchecked keep us perpetually in the dark, falling short, limited. It fosters a kind of dying, too, in the hope of giving up on old, exhausted attachments that can be replaced by an awareness that is more alive and connected. True imagination is, therefore, ground into which a person can sink the roots of their being. It proves itself through the personal experience of growth and renewal that it elicits.

Scientific discoveries arise from a parallel process, Winnicott added. The projective imaginings of scientists bring about advances when, after testing, it turns out that some of them are right. Einstein fantasized about what it would be like to travel on a beam of light. Relativity theory was the result, as was subsequently confirmed. It's why the great scientist insisted that imagination is key: "I'm enough of an artist to draw freely on my imagination. Imagination is more important than knowledge. Knowledge is limited. Imagination encircles the world."[82] It discovers what exists and, in that, experiences a confirmation that reality itself has been touched, even, that reality itself has spoken. It's one reason that science joins hands with wonder.

* * *

But there's another reason the human imagination is so important. It has a second feature. It doesn't just give shape to perceptions. It doesn't only detect reality through the fog of apprehensive confusion. It is also participative. It resonates with what it contemplates and, springing from human minds that are not just passive receivers, is active and creative in those perceptions. It's for this reason that human beings interpret the otherwise unseen world in myriad not uniform ways and, in so doing, riotously amplify and enlarge it.

At one level, it means that others not only see the same rainbow as you, but can share the same experience of uplift it prompts. We are synesthetic. Sensations are also feelings. But at another level, it means that the imagination can be revelatory. It can bring new perceptions into being. This is how metaphors work. When Jesus first said, "turn the other cheek," or, "be the salt of the earth," the experience must have been of glimpsing something not only true but daringly different. It's why his parables not only prompted the sense but created the space – in fearless, receptive minds – for the kingdom of God within.

This power of the imagination is named by Shakespeare in the conversation between Theseus and Hippolyta. Theseus makes a remark first: "And as imagination bodies form / The forms of things unknown, the poet's pen / Turns them to shapes and gives to airy nothings / A local habitation and a name." Then, Hippolyta adds that from these apparently fanciful beginnings can grow "something of great constancy" that is "strange," meaning previously unknown, and "admirable," meaning tremendous.

The second feature of the imagination was picked up by the Romantic movement, notably in Coleridge's famous summary in the *Biographia Literaria*. Yes, there is a kind of empty fancifulness that human beings indulge in. It is inventive and colorful, but you can spot it because it can only draw on what is already known to be the case. It mixes elements up, leaps from one thing to another, puts lips on chickens and wings on pigs, and is recognizable because its joys are passing, its memories prove false, and its product is ultimately confusion. And that differs from imagination proper, which is genuinely creative. It makes something that turns out to be novel and lasting, admirable and constant, because it turns out to be another reflection of what's real.

Coleridge realized that this imagination is an echo in the human mind of the creative activity of the divine mind. When the fruits of the human mind prove accurate, they partake in the fecundity of God's mind and the activity becomes another embodiment of the mystical fact of incarnation. God's creativity is born in human creativity once more. "The primary imagination I hold to be the living power and prime agent of all human perception," he began, making the same point as Kant, before adding that it is "a repetition in the finite mind of the eternal act of creation in the infinite I AM." The individual "I am" shares in the divine "I AM." That's why it warms the soul and feels so thrilling. It brings something into the world, unlike fancy that merely jumbles things up. That is its power. What was potentially there, held in the mind of God, is now seen. It's doing with words and images what God does with all that exists. The incarnation means that we are invited to become conscious of how we can share in God's life within our lives.

There seems to have been a seminal moment in Coleridge's life when he realized reality could speak in him in this way. It occurred when he saw a moonrise. He'd seen dozens before, but he was able to see this one as he hadn't been able to see the others. His imagination was ready for more. It felt as if he wasn't observing an almost daily occurrence of natural beauty but was giving voice to "something within me that already and for ever exists."[83] Seeing the Moon break over the horizon that night was more like "the dim awaking of a forgotten or hidden Truth" than it was like registering the fact that the Earth spins and its natural satellite, the Moon, therefore appears regularly to rise – which is itself quite a thought and discovery.

* * *

Others have noticed how such effects can be sparked by engaging in the imaginative writing called poetry. On occasion, it's led to nothing less than a restored love of life. The philosopher, John Stuart Mill, wrote about its salvific effects upon him after finding himself, in his late teens, depressed to the point of suicide. He discovered Wordsworth in the nick of time, and read lines like this, from "Intimations of Immortality":

> Thanks to the human heart by which we live,
> Thanks to its tenderness, its joys, and fears,
> To me the meanest flower that blows can give
> Thoughts that do often lie too deep for tears.

Mill expressed their impact upon him: "What made Wordsworth's poems a medicine for my state of mind, was that they expressed, not mere outward beauty, but states of feeling, and of thought colored by feeling, under the excitement of beauty. They seemed to be the very culture of the feelings, which I was in quest of. In them I seemed to draw from a Source of inward joy, of sympathetic and imaginative pleasure, which could be shared in by all human beings."[84] He was able imaginatively to share in the life of the "Source" and recovered as a result.

Something similar happened to Barfield. In his early life, he had become acutely depressed. In a letter to a friend, he described feeling as if he were falling in on himself "like an ingrowing toe-nail." "My self is the only thing that exists, and I wear the external world about me like a suit of clothes – my own body included," he continued. The sense of feeling trapped, as if a castaway on an island of consciousness, was for a time intolerable. But then he started reading poetry and noting its effect upon him. As he let the words penetrate his mind he saw "a sudden and rapid increase in the intensity" with which he experienced them, which in turn became a "source of delight."[85] He began to investigate the experience by attending to its quality, as opposed to trying to explain its impact. That was a crucial decision as it allowed the apprehensions to develop. "What impressed me particularly was the power with which not so much whole poems as particular combinations of words worked on my mind," he continues. "It seemed that there was some magic in it; and a magic which not only gave me pleasure, but also reacted on and expanded the meanings of the individual words concerned."

It led to a radical re-orientating of his life, a conversion, which he understood as a spiritual awakening: at base, he had been cured of a spiritual disease but he had also been born into a wider world. He realized that what he experienced was not only contained in the power of poetic words, but throughout the cosmos and nature. He concluded that words have souls, an inner vitality that, when acknowledged, can be transformative. Its magic is released by appreciating that power, and reveals a storehouse of treasures that is permanent and never ceases giving.

The revelation was profound and determinative. It was a "felt change of consciousness," as he put it. The good poet not only enables a reader to understand differently, by expanding on the ambivalences, ambiguities, resonances and complexity of things. There's another, subtler transmission that occurs as poetic words are uttered. The reader feels his or her surroundings and inner life grow. It's as if the meter and the metaphors transform the sounds into sunrays that prompt imaginative seeds to sprout. A poetic experience is both of something being disclosed and of the thrill of a disclosure itself. It takes you to the threshold of another apprehension of the world – which is why I turned earlier to poetry to evoke the experience of Plato's philosophy. "The face of nature, the objects of art, the events of history and human intercourse betrayed significance hitherto unknown," Barfield explained.[86] It happens because, crucially, poetry does not play on the surface of things, as if it were a self-referential and essentially fanciful dance. Rather, poetry extends reality because words themselves resonate with reality. They bridge and connect, and therefore, they construct and make. They are agents of creation.

Focusing on this power of words has immediate significance in a Christian context. You and I are doing nothing less than sharing, to some degree, in the work of the *Logos* when we imaginatively discern, put words to things, or use metaphors ingeniously, as if for the first time. It's a truth remembered in the myths about human beings naming creatures. It's remembered in the myths about divine speech creating: "In the beginning was the Word." When the divine source of the imaginative mind is acknowledged, the modern individual can rejoice in their share of the creativity of God. "What was first spoken by God may eventually be re-spoken by man," Barfield says,[87] which is what the psalmist was singing when he realized that God stretches out the heavens like a tent and rides on the wings of the wind (Ps 104: 2).

Barfield offered a simple example to help a reader tune into the effect. Consider the difference between how a prose writer might write, "old prophets," and how a poet would write, "prophets old." The re-arrangement alters what is conveyed. "Old prophets" is informative. It refers to prophets who lived many years ago. "Prophets old," though, has a very different feel. It is more like an invocation of the old prophets, drawing attention to who they might have been and what they might have known, and what their presence might be like now. It suggests that it's possible to recreate the spirit of the prophets; to allow them to speak in us again. The inverted word order invites the mind to open onto an expanded meaning as it admits the phrase, "prophets old."

It is this felt dynamic, generated by literary and compositional devices, rhymes and similes, that does the work. Barfield likened what these techniques do for words to the effect which is produced by the movement of wire between the poles of a magnet. The action generates something unexpected and of a completely different order. Electricity flows as a coil of wire traverses a magnetic field. There's a current, a materialization of energy, which had only been a potential before. "So it is with the poetic mood, which, like the dreams to which it has so often been compared, is kindled by the passage from one place of consciousness to another. It lives during the moment of transition and then dies, and if it is to be repeated, some means must be found of renewing the transition itself."[88] This is what poetry does. It brings into conscious being.

You could say that words contain a natural poetry waiting to be uncovered. Barfield quotes the well-known summary of this thesis, associated with the Romantic Movement, found in Percy Bysshe Shelley's "A Defence of Poetry." "In the infancy of society every author is necessarily a poet, because language itself is poetry ... Every original language near to its source is itself the chaos of a cyclic poem." To put it another way, if primordial thinking was done in the form of myths and memories, invocations and poetry, the poetic art today is one of the ways of remaking the forgotten life of our ancestors. That's part of its promise, as well.

In fact, today's composed poems and chosen metaphors are doubly powerful because they are deliberate. The contemporary writer is aware of what they are trying to do. They are letting the words speak for themselves by consciously causing the words to speak. The reader shares in the creative aspect of the enterprise, as well, which is why there's delight not only in what's disclosed but in the act of disclosure. This is a role performed by a self-conscious individual. It's why poetry is so important today. It preserves and integrates our active role as modern people in the disclosure of the inside of the world.

The same happens in the best discoveries of what might initially be taken to be poetry's opposite, namely science. The nature writer, Robert Macfarlane, is a leading proponent of the links between science and the imaginative and poetic, in relation to the natural world. He will wander for weeks, venture across mudflats, argue that our words need "rewilding," and is as at home writing about "greenwood magic" as he is unpacking the complex results of the forestry science studies he's read. He allows nature to speak back in his literary creations and argues that this dynamic has, in fact, always been part of doing science. It's another reason that science inspires so much wonder. It's nature not only entrancing us, but revealing itself once more to be enchanted. As Macfarlane explains, the tremendous realization that comes with imaginative absorption in nature is that some things can only be known in the moment of absorption. In such reveries and experiments, what's glimpsed and forged proves lasting as well as novel because something true about nature has been named.

The poetic imagination is, therefore, not just artistic, nor does it fabricate meaning from the void of an otherwise meaningless world, stresses Malcolm Guite, in his biography of Coleridge. Rather, the thrill of it is that we see operating "the very same power which itself gives nature life."[89] It is the human "I am" sharing mystically in the divine I AM. What's known is lovely but the knowing itself is divine. The same sense can be found with any text or discovery that gives and gives and gives again, each time it is encountered. The creativity doesn't cease. It's grace.

I think you particularly appreciate it in works of art when the artist disappears in the work. It's a sign that alignment with something greater has been particularly fully realized. The Bible, Plato's dialogues, the music of Bach, Shakespeare, the work of scientific genius. As Virginia Woolf observed, we probably know so little of the Stratford Bard because he lost interest in himself. He died to himself and lived for pen and stage. "All desire to protest, to preach, to proclaim an injury, to pay off a score, to make the world the witness of some hardship or grievance was fired out of him and consumed. Therefore his poetry flows from him free and unimpeded."[90] Iris Murdoch sensed something similar when she noted that the greatest art is "impersonal," in the sense that it transcends the individual person, though it's the individual person who appreciates that what's shown comes "with a clarity which startles and delights us simply because we are not used to looking at the real world at all."[91] The deliberate, liberated imagination can do that. The theist will conclude that amidst the delight the source of reality itself is being approached, Murdoch added. There is "something far more deeply interfused," as Wordsworth memorably describes it in, *Lines Composed a Few Miles above Tintern Abbey*. And note, the crucial part played by his own activity is remembered in the title with the word, "composed."

* * *

C.S. Lewis became a hugely successful creative writer, when he concluded that the rational apologetics of his earlier life could only take the communication of eternal verities so far. Lewis finally saw that truths expressed in this intermediate zone were "reality itself taking the form of human consciousness," as Barfield put it in a letter to him. Lewis himself theorized about the imagination rarely. But one case is a sermon, subsequently entitled "Transposition," that he preached at Mansfield College, Oxford, in 1949.

Like Kant, Lewis notes that all experiences have a physical and an imaginative side, with the imaginal revealing more than the physical alone could. For example, the musical notes written by Mozart are identical to the musical notes written by Salieri, if analyzed solely in terms of their acoustic properties, but everyone knows that Mozart's tunes are heavenly, whereas Salieri's are merely pleasant. Lewis concluded that it's not the sensation that makes the difference, but the felt response evoked. Mozart lifts us "higher." His soundscape is richer, more varied, more creative. That's his genius.

Lewis called this the "transposition" that the music achieves. It is its accomplishment. The notes alone are of a "lower" medium, being physical, but the music itself is "higher." It is not of the material world though it is in the world, the difference being known by its expressive or spiritual quality. A composer is assessed by just how freely and widely he or she can bring about such transposition.

A similar movement can be seen taking place in other arts. Drawing, for example, is two-dimensional but the tricks of perspective that give the illusion of a straight road receding into the distance can also give the illusion of a tower rising into the sky. The "lower" arrangement of lines transposes the viewer to a "higher" recollection of the diverse features of three-dimensional reality.

Pondering how this transposition works, Lewis concluded that it relies on the viewer, or hearer, already having some half-remembered knowledge of the higher dimension, so that the higher knowledge can be recalled upon encountering the lower. The lower participates in the higher, a sharing enabled by the creativity of the artist and the imagination of the perceiver. The flat-world of the line drawing is understood because the viewer lives in a multidimensional world. The emotional finesse of Mozart expands the emotional subtleties of which human beings are capable. The artist's skill is to channel the richer world into the poorer medium, enhancing the consciousness of their audiences in the process. It's why visual art is judged visually, not just optically; music is judged musically, not just acoustically; and spiritual experiences must be judged spiritually, not just psychologically, sociologically or materially. They must all be approached from above if they are to be understood, even if there's only a vague sense of what that "above" might be. In fact, if it weren't vague, the imaginative art wouldn't be necessary, or possible. It's also why the arts, when focused on higher spiritual domains, can carry a sense of the numinous.

This is a way to understand the relationship between mind and body, Lewis added. Mind cannot only be the movement of the brain's atoms, any more than music can only be the production of notes. Rather, the movement of the brain's atoms is the physical medium responding to the higher movement of mind. Mind is transposed into matter, as music and drawings are, and imagination transposes matter back into mind. It's a modern version of what the medieval philosophers had noted, that mind is to the brain as light is to the eyes.

If that flow from higher to lower and back again ceases, because people lose their creative imagination, the world becomes "all fact and no meaning," Lewis continued. Like Coleridge, he was onto the way in which the imagination draws the human "I am" into the divine I AM, as the higher reaches into the lower. It's a form of incarnation again, and were it to stop, there'd be just the optical, just the acoustic, just the material. "Humanity, still remaining itself, is not merely counted as, but [is] veritably drawn into, Deity," Lewis concluded. The finite shares in the infinite. Human beings find delight as co-workers, participating in the life of God. Individuality makes possible the glorious, astonishing, satisfying realization that this is so. The secret life of all things is beneath our feet and behind our eyes. We just have to turn to the imagination to see it. And when we see it's so, we share in an act of incarnation.

* * *

Few Christians have understood this better than William Blake. He was categorical. The human imagination is the "Divine Body of the Lord Jesus," he wrote in *Jerusalem*. Incarnation and imagination are identical, one seamless action. For him, as for

Lewis, that must be right because imagination alone could not bootstrap meaning out of a universe that was sheer mechanism. All that'd be possible, if the cosmos were dead, is what he called, "single vision and Newton's sleep." Only nothing comes from nothing, and if the universe were as scientism implies, even the poet and prophet would be left standing still, "unable to do other than repeat the same dull round over again." "There is no natural religion," as he put it in another place. Soulfulness can only come from divine spiritedness.

Blake understood something further. Seeing this truth fully and in all its glory requires a process of dying to yourself. This is because it's only then that we can see that our life is not really grounded in our life but in God's life. Jesus died to show the deeper way, and Blake thought of the crucifixion as necessary because people inevitably resist dying to themselves, often preferring instead "the Wastes of Moral Law." He prayed that God would "Annihilate the Selfhood in me," "to open the Eternal Worlds, to open the immortal Eyes." Then he would be free: "I know of no other Christianity and of no other Gospel than the liberty both of body and mind to exercise the Divine Arts of Imagination," he continued. The historical incarnation is a manifest realization of these divine arts, the fullness of which is known within. "God becomes as we are that we may be as he is," he summarizes in a restatement of the early Christian awareness.

He exercised this imaginative liberty in all aspects of his life – domestic, romantic, professional, devotional – because "As a man is, so he sees." We become what we are, as Nietzsche put it, so it's crucial today to adjust what you imagine you are, because it is already determining your perception of tomorrow. When a patron undermined Blake's freedom to pursue the vision, he abandoned the patron, not the vision. If that meant material sustenance was hard to come by for him and his long-suffering wife, Catherine, so be it. Blessed are the poor.

Alternatively, he developed a method of printing that integrated the way imaginative sight works with the technical practicalities of his craft. After the untimely death of his brother, Robert, he had a vision in which Robert communicated the method to him. Henceforth, he used liquids that ate away the copper of his plates to reveal his writing and designs in high relief. These contours could then be inked and colored. It was a laborious process, which explains why so few copies of his illuminated books were produced. But it was a method that operationalized his inward vision. It cleansed the "doors of perception," leaving what was essential standing out, as it truly is, "Infinite," as he noted in *The Marriage of Heaven and Hell*. With this printing method he could see reality every day before his eyes. It was, therefore, the method he adopted. Blessed are the pure in heart.

What he wrote for those purified plates was particularly fed by the participation he experienced with nature. *Auguries of Innocence* are a poignant set of such impressions. They open with, "To see a World in a Grain of Sand / And a Heaven in a Wild Flower, / Hold Infinity in the palm of your hand / and Eternity in an hour." They continue with "A Robin Red breast in a Cage / Puts all Heaven in a Rage," and, "Each outcry of the Hunted Hare / A fibre from the Brain does tear." What couplet would he have made to express the horror of the modern meat industry and battery farming? Heaven rages and the human mind self-shreds because seasons and elements, skies and insects have personality and soul, his imagination told him. When Blake said that he saw the heavenly host singing in the rising Sun, he wasn't seeing more *in* the Sun but more *of* the Sun. That's what imagination does, stresses Northrop Frye in his study of the poet.[92] To visualize is to realize, and reach towards God. That's the essence of the spiritual task today.

Blake's beliefs arose from this freedom. They carry the imprint of a theological playfulness which can capture meanings that are inclined to be lost in the dull round of creeds. For example, Blake could envisage Christ "gently conducting" Adam and Eve out of the Garden of Eden. Christ was there, though not according to the biblical story, because with the eye of the imagination, redemption is known to be timeless. Simultaneously, Blake could deny the Fall altogether because there's an element of it that feeds disparaging views of the body, and so overwrites the "human form divine." When, for example, he painted God making coats of skins as clothing for Adam and Eve (Gen 3:21), he depicted God as a smothering angel enveloping the first man and woman. If you presume God constricts and constrains with heavy doctrinal garments, you've got the wrong image of God. My burden is light.

He's tapping into the secret tradition that unveils apparently contradictory meanings which can only be seen with spiritual improvisation. It will take risks to see into the heart of God. Little wonder that Blake was drawn to the suspended end of Mark's gospel. No one has caught this moment of possibility like him, in his watercolor "The Three Maries at the Sepulchre." The three women come to the tomb and are confronted by a glowing angel pointing upward. They grip their spice jars and huddle fearfully together, eyes wide, mouths open. The scene hangs in the balance. Will the women prove too frightened to speak of what they've seen? Do they have the ingenuity to pierce the confusion? Do you, viewer, really know any better what the angel means? Can you see the kingdom?

And Blake is addressing you and me as individuals. He is clear that the message of Christianity is not fully appreciated as an abstract doctrine, universal pattern or scriptural teaching. It must be known directly in each individual heart, mind and soul because the heart, mind and soul are the true meeting places of earth and heaven, of the human and divine. That's what it is to be alive, alert and imaginative in a cosmos full of the incarnate *Logos*. "To Generalize is to be an Idiot," he wrote. "Strictly

Speaking All Knowledge is Particular."

It's an important point because it also addresses the concern that may arise from such a stress on the individual, which is that it becomes individualistic. The fear is that it risks egoism, self-obsession and disregard of others out of self-preoccupation. But Blake's individual is the "I am" who perceives an echo of the divine I AM in him- or herself, and that is not self-contained or solipsistic. Quite the opposite. This is the kind of individual who, in discovering their true nature, gets over him- or herself and so opens up to all things in wonder and love.

It's true that a narrow individualism is always a threat. The ego, as we'd nowadays say, routinely wants to possess for itself, harden its edges, and rely on its own powers of control. It's the prime and underlying cause of individuals clashing and of the loss of sight of God. But that's because the other side of the individual has been forgotten – the one that is free to know itself as it truly is, as the ground of incarnation; as the locus of the divine in human form.

So, the way to tackle narrow individualism is not to impose moral constraints upon people, as if they must love their neighbor as themselves or face the condemnation. That reduces the gospel to a set of moral instructions once more. It loads a weight upon the individual soul, and there are few ways better than this to constrain the spiritual sight which might awaken to the kingdom within. Modern human beings do not need perpetual cajoling. They do not need to be taught that they are selfish through and through. That's a sure route to fostering the kind of egoism that becomes self-obsessed with guilt, fallenness, worthlessness.

* * *

This connects us back across the history we've surveyed. As Augustine put it, we can discover that God is closer to us than we are to ourselves. Or there's the "cosmic man" of Hildegard.

She realized that human beings weren't biological specks in an empty universe but minds that can traverse the vastness. She could hear what "the Living Light sayeth" and, in that, was close to Epicurus who passed "beyond the blazing walls of the universe and traversed the immense whole with his mind and soul." Other medievals developed further images. Nicholas of Cusa spoke of God as the infinite circle whose center is everywhere and circumference is nowhere. That center can be appreciated by us in us. He described how it's found via a withdrawal from the surface of things and a reaching to the infinite aspect of all finite forms. That can be appreciated once more when coupled to the faculty of active imagination.

Early modern divines, like Blake, were onto it. Anglicanism produced some such fertile souls, as well. John Donne and George Herbert are well known. Thomas Traherne, who wrote what Lewis called "the most beautiful book in the English language," is less so. But Traherne, too, understood the imaginative vision and insisted that, "You must want like a God that you may be satisfied like a God." We receive but what we give. We can contribute to the creative *Logos*. There's an imaginative challenge.

My friend, the Traherne scholar, Denise Inge, made this phrase the focus of her study of the seventeenth-century poet. She points out that Traherne realized it is not modesty that prevents human beings wanting like a God, as if they ought to remember they are mere mortals. It's cowardice. "Unless we expect this with infinite ardency, we are a lazy kind of creatures good for nothing. 'Tis man's holiness and glory to desire absolute perfection in God," he wrote.[93] The realization of this glory comes only with the dying to self, which is why modesty is so attractive a cover story, but then it's grasped that life is not about acquiring but holding, "knowing the treasures that are before and behind us, around and within."[94] It's a paradox that participation comes when what's wanted is known to be possessed already.

The realization immersed Traherne in the wonder of nature, like Blake. "You never enjoy the world aright, till the Sea itself floweth in your veins, till you are clothed with the heavens, and crowned with the stars: and perceive yourself to be the sole heir of the whole world, and more than so, because men are in it who are every one sole heirs as well as you." It's not unlike the world of original participation except that the individual now shines star-like in it, too, as if "heir of the whole world." It's possible because of what has sprung from the watery depths of life. "I will in the light of my soul show you the Universe," Traherne continued. That's something Homer or Abraham could never have said. It's possible with the evolution of individuality and the conscious recognition that there is another world which is here.

Other Anglicans have highlighted how humanity's trio with God and nature can be sung and heard. William Law wrote: "Though God be everywhere present yet He is only present to thee in the deepest and most central part of thy Soul ... This depth is the Unity, the Eternity, I had almost said the Infinity of thy soul; for it is so infinite that nothing can satisfy it, or give it any rest but the infinity of God."[95] In the twentieth century, Austin Farrer restated things once more: "God's view is the view of mind as such, for it corresponds to the real structure of existence. The tendency of any mind, in proportion as it overcomes creaturely limitations, must be to gravitate towards the divine center, and share the divine view of things. That is the goal; it cannot be the starting-point."[96]

It's a common orientating principle in the spiritual writings of Rowan Williams, to bring us up to date. He begins a book on discipleship by, I suspect, deliberately sidestepping Blakes's "Wastes of Moral Law" and stressing instead awareness and abiding. It's no accident, the former Archbishop of Canterbury explains, that the first words of Jesus in John's gospel are, "What are you looking for?" swiftly followed by, "Come and see" (John 1:28, 29).[97] What we want to come and see is the secret.

His study of the Narnia stories summarizes the central message: it's "bigger inside than outside," one chapter title declares. Williams expands the theme:

> Just as when we meet Aslan we are put in touch with what is solid in ourselves (and obliged to let go of what is false), just as we are stripped of our private versions of reality in order to be fed with the joy of truth itself, so with our experience of the entire world we inhabit. Once we have left behind our self-centered perspective, what is opened out to us is a fuller not a smaller field of enjoyment; the world itself becomes more "intense" in its impact, and we sense (literally *sense*) dimensions to the world that we should otherwise never have encountered.[98]

The imagination is a sixth sense. It can tell that the kingdom of God is within you and lead you into the intermediate zone of Spirit.

* * *

There is a problem with referencing Shakespeare and Blake, Traherne and Hildegard, William Law and Rowan Williams. It can seem to put creative, divine imagination beyond the rest of us. They are geniuses of the Spirit. That's intimidating. But their spirit need not stand over us. It can invite us to come and play, too – "play," here, meaning to commit to the imaginative activity that brings inner and outer life together and discovers more about them both. After all, to imagine is to do nothing special. Like dreaming, to which it is closely linked, it goes on all the time. It gives form to what we perceive. It's how we see the world, according to Kant, and we all see something of reality.

The difference is that the great imaginers have learnt to let the sun of their personal perceptions set, so that the stars of a wider inspiration can come out.

It's toying with experience as if in a game. It's like learning to ride a bike or discovering the capabilities of paint. You can read a book about riding, but you have to risk getting onto the saddle to cycle. You can go to classes about painting, but at some point, you yourself have to fool around with the oil, pigment and water. Only then do you discover what the combination of the materials, your imagination and the radiance of things can achieve, and you move on from painting by numbers.

Blake embraced this transitional state of "innocence and experience," as he called it, and I think this is what Jesus meant when he said that the kingdom of God must be received as if by a little child (Luke 18:16). He wasn't saying that Christians must remain permanent kids. Rather, it's recalling that the joy of being a child is seeing the world with fresh eyes. They are not bound by received wisdom and common sense, but are alight with an open mind. Traherne caught the difference when he recalled his infant life: "The streets were mine, the temple was mine, the people were mine. The skies were mine, and so were the sun and moon and stars, and all the world was mine, and I the only spectator and enjoyer of it. I knew no churlish proprieties, nor bounds, nor divisions; but all proprieties and divisions were mine; all treasures and the possessors of them." Only later, under the guise of an education, did he almost lose such sight. "[W]ith much ado I was corrupted, and made to learn the dirty devices of this world, which I now unlearn, and become, as it were, a little child again that I may enter into the kingdom of God."[99] He regained his spiritual sight, which came back via imagination and poetry for one reason: they are attributes of the *Logos*. They take us to the heart of God.

Such play is no task. God has nothing to achieve since divine life is complete already. "It proceeds not from the seriousness and earnestness of one who strives and schemes towards a goal, but from the sheer joy of one who is himself the fulness of Being and of all possible perfection," explains Alan Watts, a philosopher best known for his writings on Buddhism and Daoism, and who was an Anglican for a time. "Speaking absolutely, God has no purpose. There is nothing beyond his own infinite glory which he could possibly strive to attain, and because he lives not in time but in eternity, there is for God no future wherein he might possess something which he does not have now."[100]

We are never wholly like this because we are partly in time not eternity. But we can consciously participate ever more in it because it is our ground. We can be translated to a different place by a parable. We can move to the threshold opened up by imagination. We can reach back to the worlds of original and reciprocal participation and wrestle with what that might mean now.

We can achieve a high degree of deliberate self-forgetfulness. In that moment, we inwardly lift our eyes. We sit more lightly to ourselves. Life stops being about what's bigger, and is instead about what's deeper. Drivenness can drop its exhausting purposefulness. Science can be set free to reveal, once more, the vitality of nature. Poetry can show its inner life; the soul can ascend on its wings. Who knows, angels may show up and things may be experienced that are in this world but not of this world. We might just stop worrying so much about tomorrow and be free in poverty and wealth. We might find that we, too, are in the world but not of the world, and recover the experience of the mystics and the secret that might still live within Christianity.

We might go so far as to lose our life because we trust that it is in dying we discover another life that is already here. It'll be known as divine life, incarnate within us. It'll be experienced in all fullness, all freedom, all truth.

Notes

1. Barfield, O. (1977). "The Rediscovery of Meaning" in *The Rediscovery of Meaning and Other Essays.* San Rafael, CA: Barfield Press, p.18
2. Diuk C.G., Slezak D.F., Raskovsky I., Sigman M. and Cecchi G.A. (2012). "A quantitative philology of introspection." *Frontiers in Integrative Neuroscience.* 6:80
3. Naydler, J. (1996). *Temple of the Cosmos: The Ancient Egyptian Experience of the Sacred*. Rochester, Vermont: Inner Traditions, p. 112ff
4. Googan, Michael. (2008). *The Old Testament: A Very Short Introduction*. Oxford: OUP, p. 52
5. Geller, S. (1996). *Sacred Enigmas: Literary Religion in the Hebrew Bible.* London: Routledge, p. 42
6. Assmann, J. (2001). *The Search for God in Ancient Egypt*. Ithaca, NY: Cornell University Press
7. Bellah, R. (2011). *Religion in Human Evolution: From the Paleolithic to the Axial Age*. Cambridge, MA: The Belknap Press of Harvard University Press, p. 296
8. Halpern, B. (2009). "Jerusalem and the Lineages in the 7th century BCE: Kinship and the Rise of Individual Moral Liability" in *From Gods to God: The Dynamics of Iron Age Cosmologies.* Heidelberg, Germany: Mohr Siebeck
9. ibid., pp. 405–6
10. See Schniedewind, W.M. (2004). *How The Bible Became a Book: The Textualization of Ancient Israel.* Cambridge: Cambridge University Press. For some more recent archeological research, see http://www.pnas.org/content/113/17/4664.full
11. "Culture Memory and the Myth of the Axial Age" in Bellah, R. and Joas, H. (eds). (2012). *The Axial Age and Its Consequences.* Cambridge, MA: The Belknap Press of

Harvard University Press, p. 388

12. Bellah, R. (2011). *Religion in Human Evolution: From the Paleolithic to the Axial Age*. Cambridge, MA: The Belknap Press of Harvard University Press, p. 311
13. Augustine, *Confessions*, X, viii, 15
14. Geller, S. (1997). "The One and the Many: An Essay on the God of the Covenant" in *One God or Many? Concepts of Divinity in the Ancient World*. Porter, B.N. (ed). The Casco Bay Assyriological Institute
15. Barfield, O. (2011). *Saving the Appearances: A Study in Idolatry*. Oxford: Barfield Press, p.130
16. Jenkins, P. (2017). *Crucible of Faith*. New York City: Basic Books, pp. 57–58
17. Snell, B. (1982). *The Discovery of the Mind*. New York: Dover Publications, p. 7
18. Colasso, R. (1994). *The Marriage of Cadmus and Harmony*. London: Vintage, p. 93
19. Jacqueline Rose writing in *The Guardian*, retrieved from https://www.theguardian.com/books/2017/nov/22/women-and-power-a-manifesto-by-mary-beard-review
20. Dodds, E.R. (1951). *The Greeks and the Irrational*. Berkeley, CA: University of California Press, p. 189
21. I'm borrowing from Barfield's discussion of this in his essay "Poetic Diction and Legal Fiction" in Lewis, C.S. (1966). (ed). *Essays Presented to Charles Williams*. Grand Rapids, Michigan: William B. Eerdmans
22. These lines from "The Listeners" by Walter de la Mare are reproduced with permission of the Society of Authors that acts as the representative for the Literary Trustees of Walter de la Mare.
23. Barfield, O. "Greek Thought in English Words", retrieved from http://www.owenbarfield.org/greek-thought-in-english-words/
24. Barfield, O. (2010). *Poetic Diction*. Oxford: Barfield Press, p.

129
25. "Sermon 2" in Meister Eckhart. (1994). *Selected Writings*. London: Penguin Classics, p. 114
26. Barfield, O. (1953). *History in English Words*. London: Faber and Faber, p. 109
27. Hadot, P. (2002). *What is Ancient Philosophy?* Cambridge, MA: The Belknap Press of Harvard University Press
28. ibid., p. 190
29. Epigram attributed to Antipater of Sidon from *The Greek Anthology*, cited by Navia, L.E. (1996). *Classical Cynicism: A Critical Study*. Westport, Connecticut: Greenwood, p. 132
30. Cited in Desmond, W. (2008). *Cynics*. Stocksfield, UK: Acumen, p. 151
31. Goodman, M. (2007). *Rome and Jerusalem: The Clash of Ancient Civilizations*. London: Penguin Books, pp. 114–5
32. Lim, T.H. (2017). *The Dead Sea Scrolls: A Very Short Introduction*. Oxford: Oxford University Press, p. 108ff
33. Jenkins, P. (2017). *Crucible of Faith*. New York City: Basic Books, p. 141
34. Barfield, O. (2011). *Saving the Appearances: A Study in Idolatry*. Oxford: Barfield Press, p. 130
35. ibid., p. 129
36. Armstrong, K. (1999). *A History of God*. London: Vintage, p. 91
37. Vermes, G. (1981). *Jesus the Jew*. Minneapolis, Minnesota: Augsburg Fortress
38. Knapp, R. (2017). *The Dawn of Christianity*. London: Profile Books, p. 125
39. Borg, M. (2017). *Days of Awe and Wonder*. London: SPCK, p. 75
40. Cayley, D. (2005). *The Rivers North of the Future: The Testament of Ivan Illich*. Toronto: House of Anansi Press
41. Jeremias, J. (2012). *New Testament Theology*. London: SCM Press

42. Dunn, J.D.G. (2016). *Who Was Jesus?* London: SPCK, p. 19
43. Barfield, O. (2011). *Saving the Appearances: A Study in Idolatry*. Oxford: Barfield Press, p. 211
44. Barfield, O. (1977). "The Psalms of David" in *The Rediscovery of Meaning and Other Essays.* San Rafael, CA: Barfield Press, pp. 277–8
45. Murdoch, I. (2001). *The Sovereignty of Good*. London: Routledge Classics, p. 30
46. Murdoch, I. (1999). Conradi, P. (ed). *Existentialists and Mystics: Writings on Philosophy and Literature*. London: Penguin, p. 215
47. James, W. (1982). *The Varieties of Religious Experience*. London: Penguin Books, p. 127
48. Dunn, J.D.G. (2016). *Who Was Jesus?* London: SPCK, p. 39
49. Augustine. (2008). Garry Wills (trans.). *Confessions*. London: Penguin Classics, p. 49
50. ibid., p. 234
51. Meister Eckhart, Sermon IV
52. Meier, J.P. "The Present State of the 'Third Quest' for the Historical Jesus: Loss and Gain", retrieved from https://www.bsw.org/biblica/vol-80-1999/the-present-state-of-the-145-third-quest-146-for-the-historical-jesus-loss-and-gain/333/
53. "The 'Son of God' and the 'Son of Man'" in Barfield, O. (1977). *The Rediscovery of Meaning and Other Essays.* San Rafael, CA: Barfield Press, pp. 285–198
54. Whitehead, A.N. *Religion in the Making*. Essay widely available online
55. Cited by Michael Parsons, "Ways of transformation" in Black, D.M. (ed). *Psychoanalysis and Religion in the 21st Century.* London: Routledge, p. 129
56. Barfield, O. (1953). *History in English Words*. London: Faber and Faber, p. 119
57. Barfield, O. (2011) *Saving the Appearances: A Study in*

Idolatry. Oxford: Barfield Press, p. 200

58. Vermes, G. (2012). *Christian Beginnings.* London: Penguin Books
59. Siedentop, L. (2014). *Inventing the Individual*. London: Penguin Books, p. 63
60. Kripal, J. (2017). *Secret Body: Erotic and Esoteric Currents in the History of Religion*. Chicago: University of Chicago Press, p. 428
61. Meister Eckhart, cited by Watts, A. (1950). *The Supreme Identity*. London: Allegro Editions, p. 83 – which Watts also notes reflects the Pauline trichotomy of body, soul and spirit, the body being the manifest element, the soul being the element that has ideas, feelings and sensations, and the spirit being the element that knows even as it is fully known, by God.
62. Harper, K. (2017). *The Fate of Rome*. Princeton: Princeton University Press, p. 156
63. Harper, K. (2013). *From Shame to Sin*. Cambridge, MA: Harvard University Press, p. 118
64. Augustine. *City of God*. VIII.4
65. Harrison, P. (2015). *The Territories of Science and Religion*. Chicago: University of Chicago Press, p. 12
66. Thomas Aquinas, *Summa Theologiae.* Question 12, Article 5
67. Barfield, O. (2011). *Saving the Appearances: A Study in Idolatry*. Oxford: Barfield Press, p. 83ff
68. MacCulloch, D. (2009). *A History of Christianity: The First Three Thousand Years*. London: Allen Lane, p. 222
69. Lewis, C.S. (1964). *The Discarded Image*. Cambridge: Cambridge University Press
70. My sense is that definitive inner change began with the Reformation and not the Renaissance, as Jakob Burckhardt famously proposed when be argued that "man became a spiritual individual" in fourteenth-century Italy. Subsequent scholarship, to my mind, has suggested

that whilst economic life began to change then, which subsequently underpinned the Reformation as a social movement, people's experience of being human didn't fundamentally shift until the Reformation. The medieval mentality of reciprocal participation still dominated to that point, being revived by, say, Petrarch's equation of knowing and loving, Ficino's interest in magic and astrology, and the shared consciousness expressed in the paintings of individuals like Ghirlandaio.

71. Roper, L. (2016). *Martin Luther: Renegade and Prophet*. London: The Bodley Head, Rex, R. (2017). *The Making of Martin Luther*. Princeton: Princeton University Press, and Ryrie, A. (2017). *Protestants: The Radicals Who Made the Modern World*. London: William Collins are new titles I've found particularly illuminating.
72. Rex, R. (2017). *The Making of Martin Luther*. Princeton: Princeton University Press, p. 229
73. McGilchrist, I. (2009). *The Master and His Emissary*. London: Yale University Press, p. 318
74. Roper, L. (2016). *Martin Luther: Renegade and Prophet*. London: The Bodley Head, p. 103
75. Ryrie, A. (2017). *Protestants: The Radicals Who Made the Modern World*. London: William Collins, p. 181
76. Heisenberg, W. (2000). *Physics and Philosophy*. London: Penguin Classics
77. Speaking on Desert Island Disks, BBC Radio 4, 10th June 2018
78. Spufford, F. (2013). *Unapologetic: Why, despite everything, Christianity can make surprising emotional sense*. London: Faber & Faber
79. Barfield, O. (2011). *Owen Barfield on C.S. Lewis*. Oxford: Barfield Press, p. 48ff
80. Cited in Ratcliffe, S. (2006). (ed). *The Oxford Dictionary of Phrase, Saying and Quotation*. Oxford: Oxford University

Press
81. See Barfield, O. (2011). *Saving the Appearances: A Study in Idolatry*. Oxford: Barfield Press, chapter 1
82. Cited in Isaacson, W. (2008). *Einstein: His Life and Universe*. New York City: Simon & Schuster, p. 387
83. Perry, S. (2002). (ed). *Coleridge's Notebooks: A Selection.* Oxford: Oxford University Press, p. 87, note 405, Saturday Night, April 14, 1805
84. Mill, J.S. (1989). *Autobiography*. London: Penguin Classics, p. 121
85. Barfield, O. (2012). *Romanticism Comes Of Age*. Oxford: Barfield Press, p. 2
86. ibid., p. 3
87. Barfield, O. (2011). *Saving the Appearances: A Study in Idolatry*. Oxford: Barfield Press, p. 145
88. Barfield, O. (2010). *Poetic Diction: A Study in Meaning*. Oxford: Barfield Press, p. 44
89. Guite, M. (2017). *Mariner: A Voyage with Samuel Taylor Coleridge*. London: Hodder & Stoughton, p. 366
90. Woolf, V. (2002). *A Room of One's Own*. London: Penguin Classics, p. 58
91. Murdoch, I. (2001). *The Sovereignty of Good*. London: Routledge Classics, p. 63
92. Frye, N. (1969). *Fearful Symmetry*. Princeton: Princeton University Press, p. 21
93. Inge, D. (2009). *Wanting Like A God: Desire and Freedom in Thomas Traherne*. London: SCM Press, p. 75
94. ibid., p. 266
95. Cited by Barfield, O. (2011)._*Saving the Appearances: A Study in Idolatry*. Oxford: Barfield Press, p. 186
96. ibid., p. 188
97. Williams, R. (2016). *Being Disciples: Essentials of the Christian Life*. London: SPCK
98. Williams, R. (2012). *The Lion's World*. London: SPCK, pp.

118–9

99. Traherne, Thomas. *Centuries of Meditation*. i.62
100. Watts, A. (1971). *Behold The Spirit: A Study of Mystical Religion*. London: Vintage Books, p. 177

Further Reading

For more on Owen Barfield:
See *www.owenbarfield.org* – A very valuable website, including articles, essays and talks.

The Rediscovery of Meaning and other essays (Barfield Press: 1977) – A collection of helpful introductory essays and talks covering a wide range of themes.

History in English Words (Lindisfarne Books: 2007) with a foreword by W.H. Auden – A fascinating summary of Barfield's work on the changing meaning of words, told through the frame of the history of these islands.

Saving the Appearances (Barfield Press: 2011) – His theory of the evolution of consciousness with discussions of ancient philosophy and Christianity, published first in 1957. A challenging but deeply rewarding read.

Poetic Diction (Barfield Press: 2010) – His earlier theory of how poetry works and the history of metaphor, published first in 1927. Another challenging but powerfully illuminating book.

Index

THE NEW OPEN SPACES

Throughout the two thousand years of Christian tradition there have been, and still are, groups and individuals that exist in the margins and upon the edge of faith. But in Christianity's contrapuntal history it has often been these outcasts and pioneers that have forged contemporary orthodoxy out of former radicalism as belief evolves to engage with and encompass the ever-changing social and scientific realities. Real faith lies not in the comfortable certainties of the Orthodox, but somewhere in a half-glimpsed hinterland on the dirt track to Emmaus, where the Death of God meets the Resurrection, where the supernatural Christ meets the historical Jesus, and where the revolution liberates both the oppressed and the oppressors.

Welcome to Christian Alternative ... a space at the edge where the light shines through.

If you have enjoyed this book, why not tell other readers by posting a review on your preferred book site.

Recent bestsellers from Christian Alternative are:

Bread Not Stones
The Autobiography of An Eventful Life
Una Kroll
The spiritual autobiography of a truly remarkable woman and a history of the struggle for ordination in the Church of England.
Paperback: 978-1-78279-804-0 ebook: 978-1-78279-805-7

The Quaker Way
A Rediscovery
Rex Ambler
Although fairly well known, Quakerism is not well understood. The purpose of this book is to explain how Quakerism works as a spiritual practice.
Paperback: 978-1-78099-657-8 ebook: 978-1-78099-658-5

Blue Sky God
The Evolution of Science and Christianity
Don MacGregor
Quantum consciousness, morphic fields and blue-sky thinking about God and Jesus the Christ.
Paperback: 978-1-84694-937-1 ebook: 978-1-84694-938-8

Celtic Wheel of the Year
Tess Ward
An original and inspiring selection of prayers combining Christian and Celtic Pagan traditions, and interweaving their calendars into a single pattern of prayer for every morning and night of the year.
Paperback: 978-1-90504-795-6

Christian Atheist

Belonging without Believing

Brian Mountford

Christian Atheists don't believe in God but miss him: especially the transcendent beauty of his music, language, ethics, and community.

Paperback: 978-1-84694-439-0 ebook: 978-1-84694-929-6

Compassion Or Apocalypse?

A Comprehensible Guide to the Thoughts of René Girard

James Warren

How René Girard changes the way we think about God and the Bible, and its relevance for our apocalypse-threatened world.

Paperback: 978-1-78279-073-0 ebook: 978-1-78279-072-3

Diary Of A Gay Priest

The Tightrope Walker

Rev. Dr. Malcolm Johnson

Full of anecdotes and amusing stories, but the Church is still a dangerous place for a gay priest.

Paperback: 978-1-78279-002-0 ebook: 978-1-78099-999-9

Do You Need God?

Exploring Different Paths to Spirituality Even For Atheists

Rory J.Q. Barnes

An unbiased guide to the building blocks of spiritual belief.

Paperback: 978-1-78279-380-9 ebook: 978-1-78279-379-3

The Gay Gospels

Good News for Lesbian, Gay, Bisexual, and Transgendered People

Keith Sharpe

This book refutes the idea that the Bible is homophobic and makes visible the gay lives and validated homoerotic

experience to be found in it.
Paperback: 978-1-84694-548-9 ebook: 978-1-78099-063-7

The Illusion of "Truth"
The Real Jesus Behind the Grand Myth
Thomas Nehrer
Nehrer, uniquely aware of Reality's integrated flow, elucidates Jesus' penetrating, often mystifying insights – exposing widespread religious, scholarly and skeptical fallacy.
Paperback: 978-1-78279-548-3 ebook: 978-1-78279-551-3

Do We Need God to be Good?
An Anthropologist Considers the Evidence
C.R. Hallpike
What anthropology shows us about the delusions of New Atheism and Humanism.
Paperback: 978-1-78535-217-1 ebook: 978-1-78535-218-8

Fingerprints of Fire, Footprints of Peace
A Spiritual Manifesto from a Jesus Perspective
Noel Moules
Christian spirituality with attitude. Fourteen provocative pictures, from Radical Mystic to Messianic Anarchist, that explore identity, destiny, values and activism.
Paperback: 978-1-84694-612-7 ebook: 978-1-78099-903-6

Readers of ebooks can buy or view any of these bestsellers by clicking on the live link in the title. Most titles are published in paperback and as an ebook. Paperbacks are available in traditional bookshops. Both print and ebook formats are available online.